This is the first thing Ray and Eunice saw following an EF4 tornado that destroyed their home.

THANK YOU, LORD, FOR THE PRIVILEGE

Eunice Redeker Hausler

Words Matter Publishing
P.O. Box 531
Salem, Il 62881
www.wordsmatterpublishing.com

ISBN 13: 978-1-953912-31-2

Library of Congress Catalog Card Number: 2021946324

Hope Lutheran School, Levittown, Pennsylvania, 1960. It was under construction when Eunice left for New Guinea in September 1959

This book is dedicated to my family:

My husband, Ray Hausler

My daughters:
Paula Meister
and
Charla Hausler-Englebretsen

Our grandchildren:
Evan and Anna Price
Aaron, Nathan, and Carlee Englebretsen

And our sons-in-law
Russell Englebretsen
and
Jerry Meister

Table of Contents

Table Of Contents

Foreword

At the beginning of time, God made something out of nothing. It seems that in our lives today, this truth still holds. God is taking flesh and blood humans, the flawed and the imperfect of society, and making a great work of them for His glory.

Within these pages you will find yourself a witness to what God can do in the life of a humble servant. As you walk through the working of His will in the life of Eunice Redeker Hausler, you will see that no earthly thing influenced these events, this life was no accident and neither is yours.

No human decision can bring us to God, but the Holy Spirit can, guiding hearts and minds in Christ Jesus. You will see how God worked to bring a small, seemingly insignificant child of the Midwest into a great adventure. Eunice's willingness to depend on God, her dedication to prayer and learning, and the talents God granted her have brought her to many lands and people.

May these pages and her story be an example of how God can guide and keep you with His Holy Will and Almighty Power. His will brings great rewards, if only we will humble ourselves to do so.

Our prayer is that this story will inspire you to trust God as Eunice has and bring you to say: "Thank You Lord, for the Privilege."

Sherry Wessel

Acknowledgments

A special thanks to Sherry Wessel, who typed the original manuscript, and Charles Redeker, who proofread the text and assisted in getting this work ready to be published.

Vital to this publishing effort was Tammy Koelling, CEO of Words Matter Publishing, LLC. Tammy and her staff exuded knowledge, grace and wisdom in pulling it all together!

Introduction

My life has been an unbelievable journey! As I write this book and think of all the wonderful people who helped me, inspired me, and took care of me physically, mentally and socially, I am filled with awe. Most of all, I thank the Holy Trinity: Father, Son and Holy Spirit for being at my side every second, filling me with faith, inspiration, wisdom and vision. And I thank God for sending His Holy angels to protect me along the way!

The reason I included so many people is because of the large number of people from around the world who inspired me and helped me and my family. God used all of these people to influence me, but ultimately He provided the courage, strength, and direction.

Included in this book, is only a small smattering of the incidents that impacted my life. To any of you who didn't get included, you are very precious to me and as long as I live, I will think of you and your many impacts upon me. I will continue to do much more reminiscing! I have volumes of pictures which sharpen the memory and bring me much joy.

My prayer is that, as you read this book, you will:

> See Jesus more clearly,
> Love Him more dearly,
> Thank Him more heartily,
> And serve Him more surely.

God bless and keep you all, until we meet together again in Heaven.

Eunice Anna Redeker Hausler

Chapter 1

Early Years

I, Eunice Redeker Hausler, was born into the Redeker family on August 22, 1934. Years before, my grandfather Johann Heinrich Redeker, came to America from Bremen, Germany to find religious freedom; worshiping God as the Bible reveals to us. He came from their home in Minden, Germany, with his wife, Charlotte, and their ten-month-old daughter, Johanna, landing in New York on September 4, 1871. They traveled across the ocean on the Deutschland, a ship with very few conveniences.

The trip across the ocean was treacherous, but they survived and landed safely. Love for adventure was in the Redeker family already then. They went through Ellis Island and applied for citizenship. They lived in a refugee house for almost a year. Grandpa had lost his money on the ship; someone stole the little he had from his pocket, so he worked for a year to get enough money to buy a train ticket to St. Louis because he knew German people there.

Upon arriving in St. Louis, Missouri, he heard about property that could be homesteaded around Venedy and Okawville, Illinois. He moved his family there and joined Ebenezer Lutheran Church. After several years they heard about homesteading land at Hoyleton. There they homesteaded one hundred and sixty-acres northwest of Hoyleton, Illinois in 1877.

Life was hard, but Grandpa worked the land farming and raising crops. He and Charlotte had eight children: Johanna, Henry, Wilhelmina, Anna, Fred, Lena, William, and Theodore. Grandpa's wife, Charlotte, died of scarlet fever on April 7, 1887, their son Theodore also died that year on July 14. One year later, in 1888, grandpa lost two more of his precious children. Johanna died on Oct 17th and William died later the same month on October 31st. Grandpa then met and married Louise Edler from Hoyleton. They married on February 28, 1889. It was hard for Louise to become a mother to Charlotte's five remaining children, but she managed well.

In those days there were no modern conveniences, so all was hard: woodstoves, growing food in the garden, canning the food, washing clothes on a board and hanging them out on a line to dry, no indoor plumbing and outhouses. In winter, laundry was hung on lines in the kitchen and dining room to dry. These were the only two rooms that were heated. Bed covers were usually feather blankets and some quilted blankets.

Johann and Louise had seven children: Martin, Richard, Augusta, Helen, Lawrence, William, and Otto (born: June 30, 1902). Life was hard with so much work! Grandpa Johann got cancer in his mouth. He went to St. Louis for good medical help, but to no avail. He died February 27, 1903, so Grandma was left to tend the farm with the children. Otto was about 8 months old at the time of grandpa's passing.

Most of the children from his marriage with Charlotte were grown; some had married or were working a job and had their own lives. My father, Richard Redeker, was the second oldest son from Johann's second marriage. He and his older brother, Martin, who was thirteen and my father, Richard, twelve, had to do the farm work alongside Grandma. Two girls were next in age and had to do a lot of the housework and cooking. The oldest daughter, Augusta, did most of the caring for Otto. There was no Social Security, so Grandma often had to help the neighbors with thrashing and other communal work. Then, when work needed to be done on her farm, the neighbors would help in return for her work. There was always a pot of soup on the stove, and more was added throughout the day, so often evening meals and lunches were soup. My father, later in life, often wanted soup for any meal.

The children were all well-educated, attending grades one through eight at the Lutheran School in Hoyleton. Grandpa was a good Christian man and a staunch supporter of the Lutheran Church at Hoyleton. He supported the school and wanted all his children to have a Christian education. Most of his people from Germany had come to America for religious freedom.

My father, Richard, was drafted into World War I and fulfilled two years of service in the army. He then married Anna Twenhafel, daughter of Louis and Minnie Twenhafel. Grandpa and Grandma Twenhafel were also hard-working farmers. They had eight children: Marie, Hannah, Bertha, Henry, Gustav. Anna, Emma, and Minnie. They lived on a farm northeast of Hoyleton. Grandpa Twenhafel was a second-generation immigrant from Germany.

Dad and Mom first lived east of Hoyleton on a farm, where Wilbert was born. Then they moved to Hoffman, where Richard and Wilma were born. Wilbert and Richard started school in Hoffman, where Dad's half-brother, Fred Redeker, was the teacher. They walked 3 miles to school. Then they moved to the Maxey place, six miles north of Shattuc, where Erna was born.

As children, Wilbert, Richard, and Wilma had a hard time traveling the distance to school. They had to ride six miles in the horse and buggy to Bethlehem Lutheran School at Ferrin, Illinois. When the family moved to Monken Place, a farm 3 miles north of Shattuc, the trip was shortened. Monken Place was three miles northwest of Shattuc and three miles northeast of Ferrin. This made the way to school shorter.

Dad rented the farm from Ed Monken of Stolletown. We had a nice two-story house with a basement but no central heating. Orville, myself, Luther, and Betty were born at the Monken Place. Orville died in infancy. Our lives were busy, as we all had to help with the farm work. We milked cows, fed the sheep, pigs, chickens, guineas and geese. We even had a couple of goats until Mom thought they were too unruly, tearing up her garden, and making messes. Learning to work was advantageous to us all of our life.

Our family was often visited by many relatives and neighbors. They would just come over anytime, especially on Sunday afternoon. Children would play games, and adults would socialize. Mom always made a meal. She had fried down meat, sour beans, canned vegetables, and potatoes in the basement. She could make a meal quickly with all the women helping. Family life was a treasure when we grew up, and it continued all of our life. My husband, Ray, and I also made our home a place where relatives and friends were always welcome.

My father, like his father, was a strong supporter of the Lutheran church and parochial school. The older children went to Lutheran schools in Hoffman and Ferrin. We had a public school, Flaherty School, about three miles from our house, so Dad let Erna, Luther, and I start there our first four years, then we also went to the Lutheran School in Ferrin to get our religious studies and prepare for confirmation in the Lutheran church. I thank God for this training.

I learned as a little child that Jesus was my best and dearest friend. When things were difficult, I could always talk to Him, and He comforted me. I remember we had to walk to public school, and the big boys would tease and scare us. I was still a little child, but I learned to pray to Jesus. He always helped me and comforted me. My mother would often read Bible stories to us, so we had a good Bible foundation already at home.

When we learn to put our total trust in God, He will continue to strengthen our ability to believe and grab hold of His promises. We can trust Him because we know how very much He loves us. God loves us so much that He sent His only begotten Son, Jesus, to restore our fellowship with Him. Stand steadfast in the promise of God and let nothing destroy your faith in His Word. His Word, the Bible, is a promise kept. God makes many promises to us in the Bible, and we can trust Him to keep each one when we believe and trust wholly in Him.

My grade school, years one through four, were at Flaherty School, a public school on Boulder Road. My father decided that I needed to start school at five years of age because I was always repeating the things my sister was learning. In my first year I rode to school with teacher, Mr. Dean Jensen, because he drove past our house on his way to the school. I had him for two years and learned many things. He had a gadget that showed us how the planets circle the earth, a real learning tool.

One morning I decided I would not go to school because I didn't like the coat my mother had made for me to wear, as I was afraid I'd be teased by the other children. She was an excellent seamstress and would take clothes from Goodwill and remake them for us. She could look at clothing in the store window and go home and make similar items for us from memory. Mr. Jensen came to the house and convinced me that it was a nice coat and he liked it. He said I should come to school because he had lots of things to teach me. He was a very kind and loving man.

During this time, my brother, Wilbert, served in World War II and we were acquainted to the hardships of war. He once came home on a short furlough and had boils on his legs and buttocks. We did not want to let him return, but he had to. We always prayed for him. As children, I don't think we realized how worried our parents were when he returned to the front lines in Germany. It was a joyous day when he came home for good.

In grades three and four, our teacher was Anna Donaldson from Carlyle. She had to drive about fifteen miles to the school. When there was heavy snow, she could not make it to the school. On those days, when we missed school, it was much enjoyed!

Flaherty School was three miles from our house. Sometimes the snow was piled high along the road, but we walked through it. Wearing a snowsuit was not always easy to do. Our school was a one-room school meant for all eight grades. A big potbellied stove was in the corner. The older boys had to get there a little early to build and stoke the fire. A small room was built on to the school where the coal and wood were kept. We often left our coats on till it got warm in the classroom. Being in a one-room school was an advantage because we learned a lot listening to the lessons being taught to the upper grades. There was a boy's and girl's outhouse along a sidewalk a little way from the school; rainy or cold, it didn't matter, you had to make a trip out there when necessary.

Twice a year, we would do plays, which was good training for acting and public speaking. We also had pie socials where the older girls in the area would make a boxed lunch and a pie. The older boys in the neighborhood would bid on them, and they would eat lunch together. Parents brought enough food for the rest of us.

In grades five through eight, I was sent to the Lutheran School at Ferrin. Pastor Alvin Marquart was our teacher. There were about 30 children in that one-room school. We now had to walk 4 miles from home to school. Often the Pastor would be called out on a sick visit, and sometimes there would be a funeral. On those days we did not have school. In fifth grade, I had only one other student, a boy, in my class. He lived farther from school then we did and missed a lot of days. When he didn't come, Pastor would not have the class for fifth grade. Because of this, at the end of the year, he flunked both of us. My father was not happy; it's the only time I ever heard him get upset with the Pastor. It all worked out okay as I was pushed a year behind, and when I graduated from eighth grade the following fall the High School bus ran right past our house for the first time.

When I was in eighth grade the church hired, Mr. David Harnagel as teacher. It was good having a trained teacher and I learned geography and science. He brought his National Geographic magazine to school for us to look at it. I spent many hours reading them, dreaming about the big wide world. Mr. Harnagel was very encouraging to me even after I got into High School. His daughter, Florence, later married my brother, Richard Jr.

Sunday afternoon visitors at Redeker's home.
Eunice front left. 1940

Richard Redeker Sr, Eunice's father

Anna Twenhafel Redeker,
Eunice's mother

Instrument used by Eunice's grade schoolteacher,
Dean Jensen, to teach the Solar System.

CHAPTER 2

High School Years

I was the first one to go to High School in my family. Dad allowed me to go, but I had to work to pay for my books, clothes, etc. This was another excellent blessing from Almighty God. He was guiding my way, and I always thanked Him for each opportunity.

I was already working at our neighbor's house on Saturdays. I was twelve years old when I started working for them. I washed their clothes, cleaned their house, and then ironed their clothes. When I got to High School, my Home Economics teacher, Mrs. Ellen Boyd, needed a babysitter after school, so I was blessed to have that work.

I enjoyed my years at Carlyle High School. Also, our church had a Youth Program, Walther League, so I knew some young people from it; I had a group of good friends and met other young people from the churches around us in Hoffman, Ferrin, Carlyle, Hoyleton, and New Minden.

During the school year, I worked for Mrs. Boyd babysitting and cleaning her house. During the summers, for two weeks, I cleaned her mother's house in Fairfield, Illinois. While there, I was made acquainted with a mission church that met in the public-school gym. It sparked a desire for mission work in me. Nora

Ernestine, a lady in this church, took me under her wing and had me play hymns for the services. I had learned to play because my parents had arranged music lessons from Mr. Schuette while we were in grade school. He came to our house on Fridays. Erna, Luther, Betty, and I were blessed with this opportunity and it served me well later in life.

I also worked a couple of summers for Helen Hochderffer, a real estate agent in Centralia, Illinois, where I acquired some secretarial skills. I stayed in town during the week with Bill and Hulda Steffen, friends of my parents.

When I was about to turn fifteen, my father decided we would drive to Texas after I got my driver's license. He wanted to visit his brother, Martin, who lived in Falfurrias, Texas. Dad bought a 1949 Buick and off we traveled. He and my mother, Luther, Betty, and I started out for Texas that summer. It was a wonderful trip and I did most of the driving. It was so exciting; the places we passed through were so interesting!

Texas was wonderful; I had never seen palm trees or the ocean/gulf so, I kept thanking God for this incredible privilege. We went to Harlingen, Texas, where Mom's cousin, Albert Twenhafel, lived. He showed us all around and we stayed with them. He took us to Mexico, where we ate in a Mexican restaurant, then to the Gulf of Mexico, where we splashed in the water. The Mexican food and scenery were such an experience! While we were there, a ship came with bananas on it. Albert bought some; for the first time in our lives, we got to eat all the bananas we wanted! Then we went on to Falfurrias, where we visited Uncle Martin and Aunt Ida.

Another highlight of the trip was that we saw the church and school at Fedor, Texas, where my Uncle Fred Redeker had taught after graduating from college. The cotton fields were amazing; we picked some and took it home as a souvenir. On the way home, we went through Missouri and stopped at the Meramec Caverns to take the tour of this popular landmark.

Our little minds were on overload. We couldn't believe what our eyes were seeing. Then it was on to St. Louis, where our Aunt Augusta and Uncle Herman Hussman lived. She always gave us special treatment when we visited her.

One evening they took us to the Muny Opera. It was so spectacular! Magnificent in its beauty. Another day we went to the Zoo, there Aunt Augusta took us to the Monkey Show and the Elephant Show. We had such a good time. Through the eyes of a little country kid, I felt I had seen the world; the trip was such a highlight. It opened windows to the world. We had Godly protection all the way as I was a new, inexperienced driver.

My Uncle Fred Redeker was now teaching at Trinity Lutheran School, Hoffman, Illinois. I was thinking of being a nurse. I took Latin, chemistry, biology; all courses I needed for nursing. Latin class was so interesting. Our teacher, Mrs. Maddux, would often get on a tangent about Greek myths. She told us about the gods and goddesses of Greek and Roman mythology. She kept us enthralled, and we wouldn't have much homework! At that time Uncle Fred started talking to me about becoming a Lutheran teacher. He wanted me to think about going to Concordia Teacher's College, River Forest, Illinois, west of Chicago. It sounded so far away. In my senior year, I started thinking about it seriously and sent in an application to Concordia.

I was immediately accepted, and my mind was boggled with leaving home, family, and preparations for college. I prayed fervently, and God made the way clear. Things fell in place so I could go. I had no money, but I was told I could get a job near the college. Two of my classmates from Carlyle High School, Agnes Michael, and Monroe White, also decided to go there.

At the end of my junior year, because of my academic standing, I was chosen to serve as an usherette for the graduating Senior class. My senior year at High School was hectic, but God just kept helping me. I graduated as Salutatorian my Senior year. I praised and thanked God for all His blessings as I felt my grade school education had not been the best; God had sharpened my mind anyway.

CHAPTER 3
College Years

In the summer of 1952, I continued working. I was still concerned about college, but God kept encouraging me through prayer. In the middle of August, my father said he would take us to college in the Buick. I have to say, my father often showed me the soft part of his heart. He said we could take Agnes and Monroe also. We packed the Buick with my Father, Mother, sister Wilma, Agnes, Monroe, myself and our luggage. It was filled to the brim. We made it to Concordia Teacher's College, River Forest, in six-hours.

Agnes and I were put in a room with eight other girls in Lindeman Hall. They were all from the Chicago area, so that was a challenge. There were two study rooms across the hall from our room. In the middle of the floor was a bathroom with sinks and toilets. At the end of the hall was a shower room with four showers. With eighty girls on our dorm floor, it was a challenge but worked out well. I was happy to have a bathroom and washroom inside; no more running to the outhouse like on the farm! Mom, Dad, and Wilma stayed in the dorm that night as some girls had not arrived. The next day, Sunday, we all went to Grace Lutheran Church, the campus church. After church, my parents left, and tears were shed.

Agnes, Monroe, and I went through four days of testing, and we all did well and then registered for classes. We all adjusted well and did enjoy our studies. Agnes and I got waitress jobs at Petersen's Ice Cream shop on Chicago Avenue, a three-block walk from campus. Tips were good, so we saw money coming in. We cleaned houses and babysat in the River Forest neighborhood as well. One particular Jewish family that I babysat for was especially good to me. They gave me extra money and several gifts of jewelry. I was not able to be in many extracurricular activities as my schedule was full. I sang in the chapel choir and joined a mission activity group. I continued to have a soft spot for missions. We canvassed new areas around River Forest to see if people were church affiliated and we were able to get many friendly responses.

I did not go home at Thanksgiving break as I didn't have money, so I worked at my jobs. I was able to make it home at Christmas on the train from Chicago to Centralia when I had saved enough money and had the time to go home. I stayed at River Forest in the summer to work while taking summer classes. I often stayed with the people I was working for when the campus was not available. One couple, Mr. and Mrs. Keehn, were especially helpful and kind to me.

My classes were interesting and exciting. I especially liked my Religion classes. The college professors and staff were very kind and showed us how a Christian family should be filled with love; they were always kind and helpful. I still remember Dr. Affelt, who taught Bible History - he made the Bible real, and I remember when he talked about Jehu, one of the Israeli leaders, he called him "the hot rod rider"! I remember Dr. Becker, who made us learn eighty Bible passages as we studied Romans. Having memorized a lot of God's Word served me well for the rest of my life. Dr. Klotz was our Biology, Physiology, and chemistry teacher, and he and his family became close friends. I babysat their children. He was serving a mission church in Wooddale, Illinois. Three male students and I went out with him to teach Sunday School.

I liked missions because it was getting the news of Jesus, our Savior, out. I had to do a diagram of the Jewish temple in Jerusalem in Dr. Hahn's class. He was impressed with my work. Later on, when I needed counseling and information to begin my teaching career, he was again a great help. My college friends, later fellow teachers, became an important part of my life and a true blessing from God. They were especially encouraging with letters and support while I was in New Guinea and throughout my life.

CHAPTER 4

Westcliffe

After two years and two summers at River Forest with no breaks from school and work, I was tired. I happened past the Bulletin Board and saw a teacher request from Westcliffe, Colorado. They needed a teacher in their one-room Lutheran School. I said a prayer - "God, I think I'd like to do this, should I?" He guided my hand to take the Bulletin Board note down, and I took it to the administrative office. Dr. Kruse met with me and said if I felt I wanted to do it; it could be arranged. This was August 5, so contact was made with Hope Lutheran Church, Rev. Otto Kretzman, Pastor.

The call was made via telephone, and they sent a contract and money immediately for my train ticket from St. Louis. I went home to Shattuc, and my parents and relatives helped me pack. My Aunt Annie Twenhafel, who was my baptism sponsor, gave me a trunk she had. It was an antique trunk about five feet long, three feet high, and three feet deep. My family helped me get clothes, office materials, and toiletries they thought I needed. My train ticket was from St. Louis to Pueblo, Colorado, with extended passage to Texas Creek up the mountain. A mail wagon was to meet me and take me into the Sangre de Cristo Valley into the small town of Westcliffe.

My brother, Wilbert, took me and my trunk to the Union Station in St. Louis, where I boarded the train to Colorado called, the Eagle. I had a sleeper car; that was nice. That night we ran into a severe dust storm in Kansas. The sand seeped into the train cars, and we were covered with it. The best I could do was brush it off, but I felt itchy and dirty the rest of the trip. We got to Pueblo at about nine in the morning. I felt like I was really in the wild west. The men looked like cowboys! The scenery was dry, and the earth was red, not luscious green like in Illinois. I did a lot of observing!

At one in the afternoon, I boarded the train to Texas Creek, up the mountain. When we got to Texas Creek, the conductor told me, "Here it is." I said, "There's nothing here, just a wood platform," He replied, "The mail wagon will be along soon."

There I was, sitting on this wood platform, all alone, with mountains and trees around me. The hour I had to wait seemed like five. Finally, a hearse looking van came along. The gentleman was friendly and loaded my trunk, complaining about it being so heavy, he said, "Lady, you sure got a lot of belongings." If he'd only known, the trunk was just half full. We drove into the valley, and it was quite a long way before we got into Westcliffe. He knew I had to go to the home of Dora Lange, as she lived next to the school and I was to board at her house. She was a widow and had her sister-in-law, Anna Lange, a former pastor's wife from Elmhurst, Illinois, living with her.

The mailman and I carried my trunk inside. I was given the front bedroom to stay in. I was not accustomed to this royal treatment. (Front bedrooms were usually reserved for honored guests!) Luckily, she had an indoor washroom, toilet, and shower. The shower that night was probably the best one I ever had! The two ladies were very good to me, and Dora cooked wonderful meals. Next door lived Marvin and Ann Rankin, Dora's daughter, with their two sons, Norman and Warren; I would become Warren's teacher. The Rankins were very good to me and treated me like family.

The next day I met with the school board in the grey, one room, brick schoolhouse. It was a rather large room with a basement to play in during winter. I would teach nineteen students in all eight grades. I was given a week to set up my room and was in charge of all school functions doing everything, including being the janitor. Thank God I had gone to a one-room school myself. I was able to handle it. Luckily the eighth grade had only one student, Arlene Hanson; she became a good friend. We correspond with each other to this day.

I had a wonderful group of students, all eager to learn. The parents were very helpful; anything I needed was given to me. Rev. Kretzman and his wife were very kind also. Once, they took me down the mountain on a road trip, not the main route 50, to Pueblo. Rev. Kretzman seemed to be a Jehu driver! His driving seemed to me like the hot rod Bible driver Dr. Affelt had described in class and I was sure we were going to fall off the road and down the mountain, but we made it safely. They toured me around Pueblo, and we ate the local food - much like Mexican food.

Throughout all my teaching years, God gave me wonderful Christian people to work with. Everywhere I went, God provided people who took care of me and showed me the sights. That was so important in my work and was a much better way to see the world rather than going on a tour. It got icy in the valley below the Sangre De Cristo range, as the temperature went down to 50 degrees below zero. The people loaned me warm clothes; I was very blessed.

Once, the Rankins took me on a ski trip up to Leadville. It was so beautiful and fun. I was not good at skiing, but I gave it my best try. In the fall, the men would go up the mountains to hunt deer. On the weekend, when they came down, hopefully with a deer each, the women would join them at the foot of the mountain for a barbecue and a joyous party. On one occasion the Rankin's and Hanson's took me up to a lake on Mt. Baldy. All the mountains had names. We fished in a mountain lake! There is nothing like it, the water, crystal clear and blue, was perfect for fishing. I caught a 10-pound rainbow trout, and I was delighted! To this day, I have trouble making people believe I caught a 10-pound fish, but I have a picture. You want good fish? - this was the best ever.

A mile east of Westcliffe was an old silver-mining town called Silvercliffe. It was a ghost town as they ran out of silver, but today it is a thriving town since many people from Denver, Pueblo, and Colorado Springs have moved up there for refuge from the big cities.

About December of that year, Rev. Kretzman took a call to another congregation. This meant, in the second part of the year, I was doing parish duties along with my usual teaching job. Pastor Riske from Colorado Springs would send up the bulletin and sermon. I ran off the bulletins and sermon on a jelly duplicator, a trying feat! The elders read the sermons for the congregation.

In January, the town had shooting matches. The range was under the tavern in town. I found it a little strange to shoot a gun, but it was another experience. I wasn't too bad at hitting targets, but of course, there was no danger of hitting a person. We also went ice skating on the local ponds sometimes, usually on Friday night. It was cold, but the towns people brought hot drinks and food; there was so much fellowship and fun.

In April, we knew the year was coming to a close. The congregation wanted me to sign a contract for another year. It was a hard decision for me and I spent many hours in prayer, seeking God's guidance. God led me to say, "No, I have to go back and finish my schooling so I can get my teaching degree."

At the end of that year, we had many picnics, a graduation service for Arlene, our eighth-grader, and a farewell party for me. There were a lot of tears. It was so hard to say, "Goodbye."

CHAPTER 5

Back to College

The Rankins drove me to Pueblo, and I boarded the Eagle back to St. Louis. No incidents on this trip. I had a short visit with my family, returned the trunk to my Aunt Annie, and then it was back to Concordia Teachers College, River Forest.

I completed my student teaching in Tinley Park, IL. They had Grades 1-4 in one classroom, and Grades 5-8 in another classroom. I fit right in since I had the one room school experience of having multiple grades in one classroom.

I immediately started summer school. I went through the next year, and next summer and got my B.S. Education degree on August 6, 1956. What a happy day! After a lot of hard work and glorious days, I could hardly believe that God was so good to me by allowing me to accomplish this. My parents, brother Wilbert and his wife, Alvira, and sister Wilma came up for the occasion. Brother Luther was working for Ozark Airlines in Chicago, so he came too. Mr. and Mrs., Keene, the people I cleaned house for, also came for the ceremony. What a special time! The evening after graduation, my dorm housemother, Mrs. Mackenson, who was known as a strict lady, gave me the key to the dorm and said I could stay out as long as I wanted to with a special friend. I knew this was an exceptional privilege because we always had to be back in the dorm when it closed at night. We went downtown to a movie, which I had never done before because I never had money or time. So many special people did remarkable things for me in my life.

CHAPTER 6

Levittown, Pennsylvania

The next thing on my agenda was to proceed with my next step in life. In May of 1956 we had a "Call night," a special night on which graduates got a Call telling them where they would serve the Lord after graduation.

The LCMS has congregations all over the United States. Those days most of them had a Lutheran School, so we could be sent to any of them if they requested a teacher from the Board of Directors of Synod.

What a blessing Concordia Teacher's College was. At that time, it was only a Teacher's college and exclusively prepared teachers for our Lutheran Schools. All students had the same goal: serving our church by being a teacher in a Lutheran School. Concordia Teacher's College and the LCMS lost a lot when Concordia Teacher's College became Concordia University. No longer are the unity and goals to serve our church as strong as they were then. When we were out in the field serving churches, we knew one another and were filled with unity to serve God, our church, and the church's children.

Then on Call night I got my Call to start a Lutheran School in Levittown, Pennsylvania, where the Rev. Walter A. Maier, Jr. was Pastor. I recognized the name from when we were children.

My father made us listen to Rev. Maier's father every Sunday afternoon as he was the Lutheran Hour Speaker on the radio. He was a founder of the Lutheran Hour.

I was astonished as I had been interviewed earlier by a call committee and told I was being considered for a call to a girl's school in North Dakota. So, I was surprised when instead I received a Call to Levittown.

I took the Call to Dr. Hahn the next day and told him, "I think this is a mistake!"

Dr. Hahn reassured me it was not. "No, Dr. Walter Maier called this week and made an urgent plea for a teacher to start a school at his church, Hope Lutheran Church, Levittown, Pennsylvania." Dr Hahn told me I was considered because of my strong character and experience in Westcliffe, Colorado. So, during that summer, I had a lot of contact with Pastor Maier and Hope Congregation.

Three days after graduation, I boarded a train to Philadelphia. Levittown was a new housing development northeast of Philadelphia; Eighty-thousand homes had been built in a short time. On the train I had time for a lot of thinking, anxiety, and prayer. When I got off the train, Pastor Maier was there with a hearty handshake to greet me. His words were welcome comfort. "So good to see you, Eunice." He said, "We are looking forward to your work among us, starting a school." He continued, "I want you to know we are equals in this work, and with God's blessings, it will be done". Then, he said in German, "Jeder Anfang ist schwer" meaning "Every beginning is hard." I understood German as it was the language I spoke until I started school. I never forgot that statement, and every time I started a new job, I told myself that. Well, my whole being was lifted up! I knew with God's help and guidance; we would get this school started.

Pastor Maier was so good to work with. He was a good evangelist and out amongst the people spreading the Gospel. The church grew in numbers quickly. I immediately had to get busy and get things organized for school. It was August eighth and school was scheduled to start on September first, just three and a half weeks away! The principals at Pennsauken, New Jersey, and Croydon, Pennsylvania, helped me set up administrative regulations. Pastor Maier already had the excitement for the school going. He already had families that would send their children to the school, and he and I visited more families to get them interested in the school. We ordered desks and school materials. The church was a spacious, oblong building. We were to start school in the basement. All went well, and we made our deadline!

The School Board decided to hire Elsie Thompson, a retired public-school teacher, to teach kindergarten. We started with thirty-two students in first and second grade and twenty in kindergarten. We had wonderful parents who greatly supported the school. The church also had an excellent secretary, Ruth Pitney, who was my right arm. Any materials I wanted to be printed, she would produce. I have to say secretaries were lifesavers for me at every school I started or taught in except Westcliffe, where I did not have one.

The schoolyear went well. Teaching two grades was a joy. We sang in church once or twice a month to keep the school in front of the people. The children really see Jesus and sing with all their heart. They relish the Bible stories and believe every word. No wonder Jesus said, " *Unless you become like little children, you cannot enter the kingdom of heaven." Luke 18:16-17*

Besides teaching and being principal, I was the organist for Sunday services, attended Board of Education meetings, and a Ladies Aid member. Carolyn Dufendach and I led the Youth Group; she carried the bulk of the load. I was also making mission calls on unchurched people, a requirement by Pastor Maier in the summer. You see, with Levittown's rapid growth there were a lot of new families, especially young families to minister to. I was delighted as people treated me with lots of love.

My salary was $260.00 a month. From my earnings, I paid $60.00 a month for room and board to a widow lady who, besides my bedroom, allowed me to use her kitchen for cooking meals for myself. Luckily, I was invited out by a lot of church members for meals. I was walking a mile to school every day. Eventually, a church member, who owned a car dealership, helped me buy a 1950 Plymouth. It was a green, two-door. It lasted me my whole time in Levittown. The Plymouth made trips to upper New Jersey, New York, Long Island, Massachusetts, Connecticut, and Richmond, Virginia, where I had friends. These were weekend trips, mostly in the summer. As counselor for the youth ministry, I took a group of our youth to a Youth Gathering in Silver Springs, Maryland, such a joyful trip. I enjoyed helping Carolyn Dufendach with the Youth Group; she was a fun person. God continued to provide good people to work with and care for me. When the car occasionally needed repairs there was always someone from the church who was willing and able to repair it. I was thankful.

At the end of the school year, it was decided to add grades three and four. The basement was getting crowded; we divided it into three classrooms separated by temporary curtain walls. This was not ideal but we made it work. We called Bessie Pakan, a Concordia graduate, to teach grades three and four with thirty-two students. We had another great year, but had no more room to add students. We decided to build a school.

We hired an architect, and in my third year, we built a new school building. It was an eight-classroom building with offices and a gym. We had terrific congregation members who helped with the construction. The enthusiasm and joy that flourished among us was a wonderful experience. I couldn't believe what was happening, so I just said, "Lord, you are Almighty, and with your guidance and power, this is possible and happening. Praise God!!!"

Dedication of the new school building, Hope Lutheran School, Levitown, Pennsylvania. December 1960

First and Second grade Hope Lutheran School, Levitown, Pennsylvania.

Grandma Ruth Pitney, Eunice's secretary in Levitown who was a stalwart in her life.

Chapter 7

God Calling

While all this was happening, God was calling me to another mission field. During the summer of my third year, I got a bad case of Asian flu and couldn't recover well. So, in October, the school board told me I should go home for a week and rest rather than go to our Lutheran Teacher's Conference in Buffalo, New York. The whole time I had served in Levittown I had not been home for a visit because I didn't have the money to do so.

So, I went home to Shattuc, Illinois, to be with my parents. It was a wonderful week. My home church, family, and friends had a lot of parties. During the week, I went to the office of the LCMS in St. Louis because I wanted material for a mission project in my classroom. My mother and my sister-in-law, Florence Redeker, went with me. I was greeted with a friendly reception at the office. They said I needed to speak to Dr. O.H. Schmidt. He asked me if I had ever thought about going to the Mission Field. I said, "No, but I'm very interested in missions." He said they needed a lady teacher in New Guinea to start a girl's school and asked if I would consider it. Of course, I was interested. He then invited me to his home that evening to see slides of New Guinea. My mother said, "No, we're not doing that." But my sister-in-law said, "Well, we can just go and look at the pictures." We did, and it was a wonderful evening. The pictures were beautiful - a mountain paradise.

When I returned to Levittown, I soon got a Call from Dr. Schmidt, asking if I would consider a call to New Guinea. I said, "Yes, I would consider it." He told me, the first male teacher serving in New Guinea was coming home in January and asked would I allow him and his wife to visit me and see me teaching for a week? I said, "Yes,"

In January 1959, he and his wife, George and Miriam Hinckley, visited me for a week. He observed me in the classroom and in other activities. They stayed with me in my house. By this time, I was living in a house with two other teachers. When they left, they flew to St. Louis and informed the Synodical leaders that I would make a good candidate for New Guinea.

In February, I got the Call to New Guinea. I prayed many prayers, talked to God a lot, and talked to my co-workers too. Of course, some thought it was an excellent opportunity, and others did not. Pastor Maier said as much as he would hate to see me leave, he felt I was suited for the call; it was a wonderful mission opportunity. I had to look up where New Guinea was and was a little shocked that it was an island halfway around the world, above Australia.

Well, my schoolyear became very busy. We were building the school where I was principal and teacher and I had to prepare to leave for New Guinea. Once again, I prayed. I can say talking to God was very comforting. No one can comfort the way He does. The peace He gave me was beyond human understanding.

We had to call a principal to replace me. We called Mr. Wilmer Kuske, who I had known at River Forest and worked with at Petersen's Ice Cream Shop. I was also good friends with his sister, Ellie. He accepted the call, so I was relieved. Then there were the farewell parties. At one of the parties was a couple from Copenhagen, Denmark, who were members of our church; the gentleman slipped a note in my pocket which said, "The love of Jesus, what it is, none but His loved ones know." That message has been precious and proven itself over and over in my life.

One member, who had been in New Guinea during World War II, asked me, "Why are you going there? It's a hell of a place!" He had been there and was very sick with dingy fever, and he remembered his war experience.

Then came the Commissioning Service to New Guinea: Rev. Herman Koppelmann came out from St. Louis to do the service. He was the Acting Executive Secretary of the Board of Missions in Foreign Countries for the LCMS. It was a very emotional May day. My parents and brother, Luther, came out for the service. The church was overflowing with people. Dr. Koppelman gave a wonderful sermon and included in it were words from Deuteronomy 31:7-8, *"and the Lord, He it is that doth go before thee; He will be with thee, He will not fail thee, neither forsake thee, fear not and neither be dismayed."* These words remained in my heart and mind as I worked in New Guinea and ever after. A delicious meal and recognition ceremony followed the service. It was tough to leave Levittown, the people had become my people, and the love, joy, and trials I experienced there stayed with me all my life. Hope Congregation didn't forget me. They supported me for 13 years while I was in New Guinea. Every six months, I received six Charlie Chip tins full of goodies: cake mixes, clothes, boxed food mixes, toiletries, anything I might need, especially Johnson's baby lotion, which they knew I used, and I have used all my life. The love and goodness they gave me was indescribable.

The Service of Commissioning

for

Miss Eunice A. Redeker

as

Missionary-Teacher to New Guinea

HOPE LUTHERAN CHURCH
Levittown, Pennsylvania

Sunday, May 24, 1959
4:00 p.m.

Eunice's Commissioning Service for New Guinea; Rev. Herman Koppelman from the Mission Office in St. Louis and Rev. Walter A Maier, the pastor at Hope Lutheran Church, Levitown, Pennsylvania, were the officiants.

CHAPTER 8

New Guinea

In June, the ladies at Hope and I shopped for things I would need in New Guinea. We packed everything and took it to the shipping dock in Philadelphia, labeled for New Guinea. I left Levittown in the middle of June with my 1950 Plymouth loaded! I went to River Forest to see my alma mater again and visit friends. Then I headed down to Shattuc to visit my family. I spent July in St. Louis in Mission School at Concordia Seminary. What a summer that was! Missionaries on leave were our teachers. We got firsthand information on life in the mission field. Rev. William Danker, who started mission work in Japan, was the primary teacher. Our class was filled with people going to Japan, South Korea, Africa, New Guinea, the Philippines, Hong Kong, and South America. This was a family builder. We left school knowing missionaries in many countries. It was a six-week intensive course, and the central theme was to spread the Gospel, the Good News of Jesus, whom God the Father sent to redeem all mankind. Our prayer was that God would use us to do this great work. As a human, I thought this was a task impossible but, knowing God would be at my side telling me what to do, gave me the courage to move forward.

The last three weeks of August were filled with last-minute

preparations, and some anxiety crept in because I was leaving America, the country I loved. God strengthened my faith in Him very much in those weeks. I even had four wisdom teeth removed during that time. I was scheduled to leave on August 25, 1959, three days after my birthday.

The Sunday before, my niece Rosalie Redeker, was baptized at St. John's Lutheran Church, New Minden, Illinois, and I was to be one of her sponsors. What a joyful day! Rosalie became God's holy child, I had a wonderful send-off from my family and celebrated my birthday, which was the next day.

On Wednesday morning, my mother, father, sister Wilma and her three-year-old son Darrell, my brother Richard, his wife Florence, and their son Charles, and my brother Luther, took me to the St. Louis airport to catch the TWA plane to San Francisco. Luther was working for the airlines. They were all in tears; however, I was not until I got on the plane and burst into a meltdown.

On the way to California, a stewardess felt so sorry for me she walked me to the front of the plane so the captain could comfort me and tell me, "All is okay, see the beautiful mountains? We'll get to San Francisco safely."

The rest of the way was better after I took out my Bible and read Psalm 23 and a couple of other Psalms. We arrived in San Francisco at 10:00 PM. Several wonderful members of the Lutheran Women's Missionary League (LWML) met me at the airport with hugs and such warm, kind words. One was Betty Raff, who became a lifelong friend. Two others also became good friends. I had two days in San Francisco and Betty and husband, David, gave me a good tour of the city: Golden Gate Bridge, trolley up and down the hill on the Main Street, Fisherman's Wharf, Chinatown, and their church. They had four children that I adored, and we walked up and down the street, telling stories and laughing a lot. The LWML ladies gave me a coin purse loaded with coins and a prayer book. Then they took me to the airport to board the Pan Am Flight to Honolulu, Hawaii.

My girlfriend from college, Eunice Merz, and several other Lutheran teachers from the Lutheran School met me with arms full of beautiful and fragrant leis. I stayed with them for two days; we had a great time touring the island. I was overwhelmed at how beautiful the world was and the idea that I would get to see it. They took me to a luau and evening performance of native dance and culture.

From Hawaii we had a stopover for refueling in Fiji. This was my first experience with islanders, and my mind was filled with wonder and awe. While they were refueling the plane and preparing for flight, we had a chance to look around. The vegetation and foliage around the airport there was beautiful, a tropical paradise. We left there and went on to our destination in Sydney, Australia, where I was met by Mr. Hamer and his wife from Nelson and Robertson Co., our mission's company to deal with for shipping and greeting missionaries. I had to stay in Sydney four days before I could get a flight to New Guinea.

They took me to the Occidental Hotel. It was not modern. You got a room and had to walk down the hall to a shared washroom/bathroom. I felt a little lonely and maybe afraid, but the next morning I ventured out and found a Lutheran church. They had service at 10:00 AM, so I went to it. The service was so much like ours at Bethlehem Lutheran in Ferrin, Illinois: it lifted my soul. I knew God was with me. My faith revived. I knew He was always with me, and I was serving Him. He gave me great courage.

That afternoon Mr. Hamer came to the hotel and asked if I wanted to stay with them; they thought I might be lonely. Of course, I accepted. I found them wonderful, but their speech and ways of doing things were a little different than in America. They had a modern home with an indoor toilet and bathroom. They gave me information about things to see and where to go. I did some sight-seeing on my own the next day. I visited the Sydney Zoo, harbor bridge, and saw some stores but didn't buy anything as I already had enough luggage. The movie, My Fair Lady, was on at 2:00 PM, so I went in to see it because I'd get out before dark to walk home.

I was having a challenge getting used to Australian money; their pennies were as big as our half dollars. I always gave them pound money so I'd get change. By the time I was going on to New Guinea, I had a heavy pocketbook of change. Pounds, shillings, and pence were their money.

On the last day, Mr. Hamer took me to the airport. I was to catch the TAA plane to Port Moresby, a coastal town of Papua. Papua and New Guinea were not yet united at this time. I listened to the announcements but never heard TAA; all I heard was TII, so I went to the counter and asked the lady about TAA. She said, "You mean, TII? Well, honey, it is ready to leave. Here come with me, and I'll quickly get you on the plane." Thank God she helped me get on that plane, or I would have had to wait a week to get a flight to New Guinea.

We flew along the coast of Australia. I saw a lot of ocean on one side and land on the other. We landed in Port Moresby at about 2 PM., and I made my first acquaintance with the natives. They were uneducated and primitive, but an amiable people.

My next move was to a DC-3 aircraft, left behind from World War II. It had a row of seats on each side of the plane with cargo in the middle. Well, it got up in the air headed for the Highlands, Mount Hagen. A little bit into the flight I saw cracks in the doors, you could see outside! I said, "Lord, please grant this to be okay."

I was sure we wouldn't make it to Mount Hagen, but we did. There we landed on the grass. I was to wait until another Mission Aviation plane came to fly me to Wapenamanda, our mission business station. I waited for an hour, and finally, it arrived.

The pilot was a very kind, friendly man. Mission Aviation Fellowship consisted of men who were flying on the island during World War II. After the war ended, they had decided to come back and fly missionaries to the Highlands. They hoped this would help, educate, and teach the Highlands people, as they learned about the Bible and their Savior Jesus Christ.

The flight to Wapenamanda was beautiful, the sun shining on the mountains and valleys as we flew over. I remembered Dr. Schmidt's words in the mission office in St. Louis. He said, "The highlands of New Guinea are an eternal paradise and spring." The Western Highlands was where our LCMS missionaries worked. We came there by request of the American Lutheran Church who didn't have the manpower to work there. So, they asked the LCMS to come in. So, when the LCMS decided to move into the Western Highlands, they decided to address the needs of the "whole person," as the people there were primitive and never had had any contact with the civilized world. We workers weren't going in to just evangelize, but to provide medical help, educational training, agricultural instruction, vocational skills and construction equipment, hygiene training, nutritional education (the people suffered from the lack of protein, salt, and other nutrients), and clothing in order to address the multi-faceted needs of the whole person. Years later after assessing the many mission fields of the LCMS, the work done in New Guinea was considered a very successful mission.

In 1948, two young seminary men, Rev. Willard Burce and Rev. Otto Hintze, along with Rev. Harold Fruend, an Australian missionary, and a fourth man who was a carpenter, walked into the Western Highlands and set up a station at Yaramanda. To read their story, read the book Otto Hintze wrote: "From Ghosts to God in Enga Land," available on amazon.com.

The plane landed at Wapenamanda on a grass airstrip. A lot of New Guineans had gathered as they always did when a plane (balus) landed. I got off the plane, and they gathered all around me; some started reaching for my head. I had worn a hat of peacock feathers, made by our neighbor lady that I use to work for, Blanche Noller. I was a little startled, but I saw a motorbike coming down the road, assuming it was our business manager, Ed Dicke, and it was. Several other staff also arrived, and I got a hearty welcome.

They put me and my luggage in a jeep, and we rode to the business office. Phyllis Dicke, Ed's wife, invited me over for a cup of tea as I was waiting for a jeep to take me up the valley to Yaibos, where I was to stay with Rev. Ian and Enid Kleinig and their four children. Plans were that we would start a Girl's School at Yaibos. The ride up in a jeep was a rough, dusty experience - but "Hey, I'm in New Guinea."

The Kleinig's were a loving family. I moved into a spare bedroom they had. Two other workers, Roland Fruend, an agriculturalist from Australia, and Walter Schmitt, a carpenter from Canada, lived in a bush house in their yard. They also ate at the Kleinigs', so Enid Kleinig had a good supper (called "tea" in Australia) for us all: roasted potatoes, carrots, beef roast, and homemade bread, with cherry tarts for dessert. She had New Guineans helping her cook for such a group. All the cooking was done on a wood-burning stove. I was thinking, "Well, what a delicious meal together, it's not too bad." I slept well that night; I was exhausted.

The first weekend I was there, I went to Amapyaka, a mile

up the road, where our missionary children went to school. There was a nice school building and a boarding house building where caretakers from the U.S. and the children lived. They had to come and stay for the week before going home (boarding school). Boarding away from home at such a young age was hard, especially for the little ones in grades one and two. Don Gerber was the principal, and they had several teachers, dorm parents and helpers who lived in the dormitory.

That weekend, on Sunday, I climbed over two mountains with the Kleinig's to a baptism. Pastor Kleinig had instructed the people of this village in the Word of God, and they were ready to be baptized. What an experience! The people had been taught for almost seven years so the missionaries were sure they knew God the Father, Son, and Holy Spirit and did not have Him connected to the spirits they had worshiped before hearing God's Word.

The people being baptized were dressed in white clothing, a cotton material from Hong Kong wrapped around their bodies; they called it a lap-lap. White signified all their sins were being washed away, and they were becoming God's holy child. They marched from a house on the hill to the bush church, where the seats were logs to sit on. The walls of the house were made of woven grass and the ceiling of bundles of grass. They sang all the way down the hill to the church. You can imagine how awed I was. I knew I was in the right place as I felt God's presence as never before.

Rev. Kleinig had a wonderful service with the New Guinean assistants. It was in the Enga language, and I understood very little, but I was so inspired. After the message, the people were baptized. It was such an exciting-praise day! After the service, the people had mummed food (food cooked in banana leaves in a pit on hot stones, covered with dirt for about 6 hours). We had sweet potato, pig meat, and some greens they picked along the road and all around their gardens. They opened the pit, and we enjoyed a delicious meal together. Banana leaves were our plates. We all had a bottle of water with us.

Then we walked back to Amapyaka and rested at the Gerber's. The walk was very hard for me as I was not acclimatized to the altitude, 6000 feet above sea level. Suddenly there was a terrible noise! Some New Guinea boys and a son of our mechanic, Lou Heppner, came screaming up the hill. The Gerber's son and one of the Heppner sons had jumped in the river. The Lai River was treacherous; it ran from the top of the valley down the mountain for miles and miles. Well, we all ran down to the river and could not see the boys. We walked a long way down the river, but no sign of the boys. We were all crying and in shock.

Later that evening, some New Guineans found Donnie Gerber; he was five years old, but he was not alive. The Heppner boy was 7 years old; his name was Ivan; he was not found. So, we were grieving and praying. Clem Janetski, our mission carpenter, made a box to put Donnie in. His wife, Esmay, and I fixed up the body. I had some new bed sheets that we laid him on. The next day we had the funeral and buried him at Amapyaka. It was a heart-wrenching experience.

A week later, the New Guineans found Ivan far down the river. They brought him up, and we did the best we could to fix him up. Clem Janetzki again made a box, and we had another somber funeral service. We buried him next to Donnie Gerber. We all needed the comfort of God's Word after this happened.

As we ran down to the river, I got a nasty scratch on the inside of my lower left leg; in a few days, it got very infected. I went to the mission hospital at Mambisanda to see Dr. Klomhaus, our mission doctor. He said, "You have a tropical ulcer." It sounded bad to me. He cleaned and bandaged it and said, "Come back in five days." I went back, and it was no better; tropical ulcers are hard to heal. So, he decided to put sulfur powder in the hole it had made in my leg, bandaged it tightly, and said "We won't open it for six weeks." Of course, I wondered about this, but when I went back, he took the bandage off, and it was healing well. So again, thank you, Lord, and thanks for a Doctor who knew what to do.

On Monday morning, I visited a school with Enid Kleinig, teaching about twenty small children at the Yaibos station. She was teaching in Pidgin English, a language brought in by German traders along the coast. Some New Guineans had learned it from coastal teachers who came up from the Lutheran mission at the coast to help us. Our mission staff all learned it quickly as it is an off-take of English.

The people in the Western Highlands spoke Enga. That was the language to learn in order to really communicate with the people of New Guinea. I learned some Enga, but since our teaching was to be in English, I only knew enough for conversation. New Guinea was under the United Nations jurisdiction, and they were making it an English-speaking people.

I helped Enid with her teaching and was learning to know the people. They did not wear traditional clothes. The women wore grass skirts, and the men wore beaten tree bark held up with a belt woven of reeds with grass leaves at the back. The children wore nothing, so the mission gave each child a lap lap (a piece of material wrapped around their waist).

Getting acquainted with the New Guineans and their lifestyle was critical to my being able to work with them. At first, I had a hard time. The women lived in a long bush house with the pigs and children. The men lived in a smaller round bush house.

As you entered the house, there was a fire built in a hole in the ground floor for cooking their sweet potato. Their diet consisted of sweet potato, and they'd pick some green leaves that they knew were good along the paths where they walked. The women had only a front entrance; if a fire got out of control in the front, they and the children and pigs would burn up; there was no way out.

I had a hard time with their way of life; it seemed so primitive to me. Some things you hoped could be changed. They made gardens so they would have food. The men would do some cultivating with bush knives and axes and then made mounds. The women planted the sweet potatoes on the mounds. That was the successful way to grow sweet potatoes.

Eunice leaving for New Guinea- St. Louis Airport- September 9, 1959
Front- Darrell Maschoff, Charles Redeker
Back- Richard Sr. and Anna, Wilma Maschoff, Florence and Richard Jr, Luther

Papua New Guinea

43

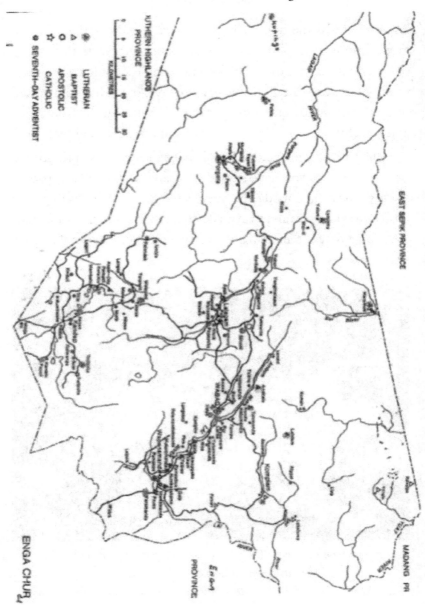

Papua New Guinea
Enga Province
Western Highlands
Lai River Valley
Where they worked

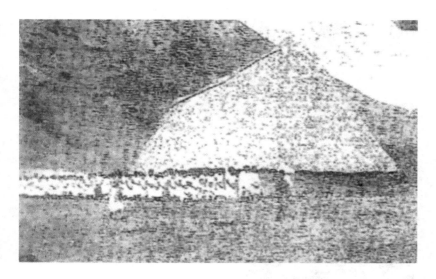

Large baptism at Yaramanda, Western Highlands, New Guinea, 1957 Church- grass roof.

Woman carrying her sweet potatoes to market. They carried their children in a billium (string bag made from hemp plant) Also used these for heavy foods and cargo.

*A woman working in her garden,
planting sweet potatoes.*

The "Te" Festival-when pigs were exchanged, and debts settled for the year.

A lady's bush house. She had the children and pigs living with her.

Chapter 9

Girl's School

When the children came to school, we made them wash at the river or stream because they had no place to bathe at home. We supplied them with clothes, loincloths, or lap laps for the boys and long blouses for the girls. Teaching was very basic as they had no contact with numbers or the alphabet. So, we wrote Math books: small pocket size English books were supplied by the government. You had to be very creative as a teacher. We had to make everything needed in the classroom.

Eventually, our mission business and supply shop at Wapenamanda got paper, pencils, and poster board to make posters. What a joy to get those supplies! We also got lined paper eventually; until then, we would make it sheet by sheet. We got some storybooks from the coast, Madang, Lae, and Port Moresby, where education was at a higher level.

I was preparing to start a Girl's School, which meant a building, desks, and equipment to start a school.

We had a good boy's school at Pausa, a station down the valley about fifteen miles. One day Rev. Burce stopped at Yaibos. I said to him, "Is there a possibility we could have the girl's school at Pausa with the boys? That way, all we need is a dormitory for girls and a place for me to live." He thought it over and discussed it with several other missionaries because co-education was not done on the island.

They decided to send me to mission stations at the coast; Madang, Finschhaven, Lae, and the island Siassi. I flew out there and spent time at several mission stations and schools. The consensus was that they were starting co-education at their stations as it would be a saver of space and manpower. While I was at the coast, I took a mission boat, the Simbang, from Madang to Finschhafen, an overnight ride; Dr. Klomhaus, our mission doctor, and his wife were on it. They were at the coast vacationing. We had a mission house in Madang, and all missionaries were allowed a two-week vacation there once a year. It was such a beautiful coastal town and had a few Chinese merchants who had moved in and opened stores. They were filled with all kinds of interesting items like clothes, dishes, trinkets, etc. We all enjoyed shopping in them. The American Lutheran Mission also had an import/export store there, Lutmis, and we were able to find things we had run out of and take them home because there were no stores in the Highlands.

I loved Madang. It was my first time to eat tropical fruits like pawpaw, mango, breadfruit, a large grapefruit that was very delicious, and coconuts. The beautiful palm trees, flame trees, frangipani bushes, and tropical vegetation were heavenly even though it was very hot. On the Simbang, a medium-size boat, Dr. Klomhaus said to me, "Did you ever dream one day you'd be floating on a boat in the South Pacific?" I was so blessed to have this opportunity. Finschhafen and Lae had many sunken ships in the harbor plus other relics from World War II. The missionary families treated me royally and shared so much educational information with me. When I was in Lae, the arrangement was made for me to visit the Australian Lutheran School on the island of Siassi, an overnight ride from Lae.

I had to ride in a medium-size boat, the Umboi. It was very crude. They had two men to operate the vessel; two others were aboard also. It carried supplies to the Australian Lutheran missionaries on the island. The waves tossed the boat around a lot, so I had very little sleep. The bed was a wooden plank with a pillow. Mr. Heinrich, the captain, was very kind. He put a trawler behind the boat to catch fish. They caught one and cooked it for breakfast along with a can of spaghetti. I was definitely in another world.

When we got to Siassi about 10:00 AM, Rev. Eckerman and some of his schoolboys met us and took me to their house. I stayed there five days until the boat came and went back to Lae. My stay was enjoyable. Mrs. Eckerman was an excellent cook and made delicious Australian dishes and desserts. Their desserts consisted of fresh fruits, Jell-O, canned fruit, and homemade ice cream, all covered with a good helping of custard.

I learned so much from the way Rev. Eckerman handled his students and his curriculum. His boys (no girls yet) could sing beautifully. You could start a hymn or song, and they would immediately break into four-part harmony. It was heavenly. In the evening, we sat on their verandah and sang hymns, such a faith-strengthening experience for me. I knew then that God had called me to a beautiful place, and I was going to love the people just like Mr. and Mrs. Eckermann did.

One night the boys took me in a boat to go spearfishing. It was such an experience! They would turn on their flashlights, and the fish came around the boat, and they speared them. We caught two buckets full and cleaned them. Then, Mrs. Eckerman and her kitchen help cooked them for dinner the next evening. All the students came to join us for dinner.

About the third day I was there, Rev. Keith Nagel from the other side of the island where he and his family were stationed came over with his boat with half of a cow dressed and ready to eat. Some of his boys had gotten hungry and killed one of their cows. They could only use half of it since there was no refrigeration; it had to be eaten quickly. When he went back, he took me along to his station, and that afternoon some of his men took me in the boat to an island, Amarat, about an hour ride. The island is known for its beautiful shells. It was a remote island, no people, but oh the beautiful shells! They helped me pick up some beautiful ones, which I treasured and brought back to the U.S.. Then we went back around the island, and Mr. Heinrich had made the trip back from Lae and was ready to go back.

The rough ride back was a little more comfortable since I knew what to expect. In Lae, I visited schools and got more information, so I was ready to go back to Yaibos and start my own school. God had given me such a rich experience. When I got back, I reported to Dr. Burce and the other leaders in our mission that co-education was starting to be common at the coast. They said, "We'll move you to Pausa" where a boy's boarding school was in operation. The boys' school was started in 1957, and girls would now be added in February 1960.

The schoolyear there is from February through November. December and January are holidays. They would build a dormitory for girls so they would have everything needed to start school, including books and other supplies. I lived in Dale and Lucy Busse's living room. The house was made of corrugated iron. They built the girl's dorm behind where my house was to be. Dr. Koppelman, mission executive from St. Louis, Missouri, came out for an official visit. He said they needed to build a house for me soon and after 3 months they did. I loved it!

Dale Busse and Ken Bauer were the teachers at Pausa. They had two bush classrooms and two permanent classroom buildings - tin roofs and Masonite siding. These classrooms were airier and easier to clean than a bush classroom.

It was quite a task to get some girls to come to school as they would then not be available for marriage at an early age. Girls were to get married at age thirteen or fourteen to bring in money for the "bride price." The boy's tribe would have to pay a lot of pigs to the bride's father to marry his daughter. If the girls went to school, they might not come back to marry. So, we did a lot of visiting the mission stations, and we got seven girls for the first year: Yalyowan from Yaramanda; Tindiwame and Kegeme from Raiakama, ten miles away; two from Yaibos, fifteen miles away; and two from Sirunki, forty-five miles away; these were our mission stations. I had to be a "mother" to these girls.

Besides the classrooms, there were three boys' dormitories, with about twenty in each dorm. I had to write books for the girls about cooking, sewing, personal hygiene; and Social Studies for both girls and boys.

Dale and Ken thought the girls and I should do the cooking for the boys so the girls could learn cooking. Two meals a day were served. We boiled sweet potatoes in big pots. The children didn't like this method so much as they were used to cooking their sweet potato in the ashes of their fires. Cooking was a lot of work for the girls, and they had to get to class on time. We were getting up at five AM to meet our schedule. After three weeks, I got very ill, I was exhausted and had malaria, but the Doctor couldn't diagnose what was wrong. They thought I was maybe suffering mentally or in severe depression.

Finally, Dr. Klomhaus sent me to Madang to Dr. Brown, a tropical Doctor. He examined me and immediately found a big lump in my spleen, as big as a baseball. He said, "You have chronic malaria!" and I said, "Good, I have something!" I could not stand the concept of being a mental patient. Dr. Brown put me on 3 different anti-malarial medications for fourteen days, and I healed. After three weeks, I was able to go back to the Highlands and my work. We made a schedule for boys to help cook meals, so the girls and I were only on duty for several meals a week. This helped relieve stress for the girls and me.

It was hard for the girls to adjust to living in a dormitory. This was also hard for the boys, so we teachers spent a lot of time with them. We did a lot of praying, counseling, and singing hymns and folk songs in the evening.

We had water tanks built next to the dormitories to catch water for their use when it rained. It was needed for drinking and bathing.

I was always so busy I had little time to feel lonely or homesick, although I did miss the people at Levittown, my family, and the U.S. in general.

Mail took two weeks to get to the U.S, and two more weeks to get an answer. As I got to know the people and students in New Guinea, they became my people. I saw that they were also God's children, and we were there to teach them the Bible, the good news that Jesus was their Savior, He loved them and died for them also. They soon learned love and thrived on it. Our classrooms were full. However, we sometimes started with ninety students in a room in February, but by July, we would be down to fifty. School life and education were not something they wanted to do, but after a while, more and more of them saw that education was a good thing. Our students were graduating and going to good jobs that brought them money, adventure, and a better life.

We teachers had to be creative always and do new things. We had the students build a cricket field, on which they could also play baseball, soccer, field hockey: mostly Australian games.

At this time, New Guinea was under the United Nations' jurisdiction, and they delegated Australia to take care of New Guinea.

In 1981, New Guinea and Papua gained their independence, and the two parts of the eastern side of the island, Papua and New Guinea, were joined and were called Papua New Guinea or as we call it PNG, with Port Moresby as the capital.

Our school at Pausa grew; we added more classrooms and housing for students. We eventually became St. Paul's Lutheran High School. We had Standard level (elementary grades in the U.S.) schools at each mission station, and they would send their graduates to our school. Many children did not go to school initially, but eventually, more and more did.

The roads in the valley where we worked were dirt paths, so building better roads was a constant process. Men would make roads with their tools: stone axes, and stone knives, which was difficult work. The women had to carry stones from the river in billums (bags woven from pit pit, a hemp plant). They had many covered bridges over the streams. It was hard, back-breaking work.

The mission was then able to buy a jeep for each mission station. Traveling up and down the valley became possible. Later in 1966-67, the government brought in the Dillingham Company from Hawaii to build roads. Before that, the roads were dangerous, and a trip to Mt. Hagen would take a whole day. After Dillingham came in, the roads were like superhighways, and a trip to Mt. Hagen was four and a half hours. Traveling over the mountains takes a little more time. The missionaries used motorbikes a lot at first. I even had one, but they were dangerous when the roads were wet. Once my bike slid, and I got a bad burn on my leg. It turned into a tropical ulcer again and took a long time to heal. I got Dr. Connor, our new Doctor, to put two tablespoons of sulfa powder on it, as my doctor had done previously, and bandage it. It was left on for six weeks. When he took it off, it was healed! Thanks to Doctors who knew tropical medicine and our God in heaven Who healed.

Our mission was growing! We were adding more mission stations up the Lai Valley and into other areas that we had to fly to or walk over several mountains to get to, like Maramuni, Kopiago, Pogera. etc. That was a big ordeal as airstrips would have to be built, and a mission house and a church also would be built. We were always able to get New Guinea men to carry our cargo.

My mission call was for five years. After I was there two years, the mission decided that single people could go home after three years of service. I started making plans for my trip home in the third year. Reta Wiebe, one of the nurses, was my good friend. We often got on the same motorbike and ventured up the valley to visit fellow missionaries. When the mission was started, the leaders decided to take care of the people spiritually and physically. They started a hospital at Mambisanda, close to Wapenamanda (business headquarters) and across the valley from Pausa, where our school was. We had a Doctor, pharmacist, and four or five nurses at the hospital. We also had a medical station at most mission stations supplied with a nurse. The hospital was built to handle many patients, with six or seven wards; each ward had thirty to forty people. I would often spend a weekend with the nurses. We had highly qualified staff at the hospital. Eventually, we had a surgeon on staff as well as a medical Doctor. New Guineans would carry patients on a stretcher made from two bamboo poles held together with strong vines. They carried them to the road, and then a jeep picked them up and drove them to the hospital. Patients were brought down from all the mission stations in jeeps if it was too far to carry them. The mission staff was also cared for at the hospital.

To: Mr. and Mrs. Ray Hausler,
The Graduates of Lae School of Nursing- June 5, 1968
Name and District which we belong to, from right to left:
Back Row: Hane Mase (Port Moresby), Alice Kulunias (Rabaul), Rhoda Ase (Daru), Mary Momel (Manus Island)
Front Row: Ruth Annam (Lae), Darusila Vaiut (Rabaul), Tindiwan Maua (Wapenamanda), Kegeme Minao (Wapenamanda), Agnes Mapes (Kavieneng), Francis Pohn (Rabaul).
Love,
Kegeme and Tindiwame
Two of the first girls in Eunice's class at Pausa when she started Girls Education.
Kegeme and Tindiwame are the two girls in front center.

Reta and Eunice riding on Reta's motorbike. Eunice also had one.

*Reta and Eunice with twins. Usually, one was killed as
the mother could only feed one.*

Women going to work on the road, they carried heavy stones from the river up to the road in their billiums (string bags made with hemp)

The second year of girls attending school at Pausa. View behind Eunice's house.

CHAPTER 10

Furlough #1

So Reta and I worked on our trip home. Ed Dicke, our business manager, was very helpful and made most of the contacts. We made travel arrangements with Orbit Travel Company. It was a super trip itinerary! I would fly to the island of Biak, Manila (Philippines), Hong Kong then, board an Italian ship to Naples Italy, with port stops at Singapore, Calcutta (India), Colombo (Ceylon, now Sri Lanka), Bombay (India), Karachi (Pakistan), Aden (Yemen), Suez, (while the ship went through the Suez Canal) we would continue with a bus tour through Egypt, see the Nile River, Cairo with the pyramids, and Port Said to catch the ship again. We were then to fly to Jerusalem, and on to Naples Italy. But in reality, we had to skip Jerusalem and go straight to Naples because of the war in the Holy Land. We would get off the boat, but before we did, we would arrange for most of our luggage to go on to London and be sent to the Queen Elizabeth II. We only took a small carry bag and our winter coats with us. We had a train ticket to Paris and London, but we never used it as we stayed at Youth Hostels and found out we could see a lot more if we hitch-hiked. Then we had our boat trip on the Queen Elizabeth II back to New York. Once we had this trip organized, we were excited and thanked God for being so good to us. So, we finished our work until the day we left New Guinea. It was hard to leave, there were many tears and hugs that I did not want to end. We had developed a very close bond with the New Guineans. All those we had been with knew Jesus as their Savior, so our hearts were joyful.

Reta left two weeks earlier than I did. She went to Australia for a family visit and to see a young man, Philip Thiele, whom she had met on an earlier trip there. She got engaged to Philip during this trip. I left Wapenamanda for Lae and then to Biak. It was a hard flight, as I knew I loved New Guinea. It was great to see Reta in Biak. Biak is an island above Dutch New Guinea, the other half of the New Guinea island. Dutch New Guinea is now a part of Indonesia. Biak was built up as an air force base in World War II. We flew KLM, a Dutch Airline, to Manila, Philippines. We were met by missionary families; some we had met in Mission School in St. Louis. They treated us like family immediately.

We stayed with Reverend and Mrs. David Schneider. They and the other missionaries took us all around Manila. We rode the jeepneys (left over jeeps from World War II) and bicycles with carriages on the side for riders. It was very crowded everywhere. We loved the markets with all the foods they grow, lots of materials, clothes, trinkets, shells, and shell ornaments, and everything was so colorful. I kept thinking, "Dear God, thank you for the privilege of letting us come here." But I kept saying this prayer everywhere we went! We went up to Baguio, where the school for pastors was. Also, we visited schools mostly in bush buildings, but the children were learning. They sang beautifully for us, mostly Christian songs. They were shy but happy. We went to Mindanao in the mountains, where Pastor Becker and his family were. Their station and work were similar to how our stations were set up in New Guinea. They made delicious food for us everywhere. I especially enjoyed the lumpia, like egg rolls but mostly vegetables inside.

The people were so friendly, and we learned to love them quickly. They gave us gifts of shell necklaces and bracelets. One night at the Schneiders home, I was sleeping in my bed. They had put an insecticide candle by my bed to keep the mosquitos from annoying me. For some reason, I was restless and threw my pillow on the floor. It landed on the candle, and I woke up to a small fire by my bed. It got the whole household up to help put out the fire. Fortunately, it didn't do much damage, but I was upset badly. I had very little money, but I gave them a small compensation to fix the damage.

Reta and I also went to a beauty shop to get our hair done; what an experience. We had a lot of teasing of our hair and poufy piles on our heads! It was something we had never done as we did our own hair. After a week, we had to move on. We had made many good friends, and a lot of tears were shed again.

We flew on to Hong Kong. Mrs. Thode and Reverend Hinz met us and took us to Ruth Profts house. She invited us to stay there as she had gone to New Guinea and stayed at my home there. Mrs. Thode had lost her husband but was still working there. The missionaries there showed us a wonderful time.

Rev. Hinz took us to the city and over to Kowloon. We ate in a lovely and beautiful restaurant and had our first acquaintance with many Chinese dishes. Martha Boss and Gertrude Simon, nurses in Hong Kong, took us to the TB hospital and the school where they were nursing and teaching. Also, we went to a church service there.

Gertrude was continually handing out Gospel pamphlets. They showed us a very crowded housing complex, ten people living in a room. It was so crowded everywhere you went. They took us to the large mission school there. We praised God for the many people being reached with the Gospel and how joyful they all were.

Hong Kong is a beautiful city, with so much to see, also at night. We ate at exquisite restaurants, saw an acrobat show, and went to a tailor where we had two dresses, shoes, and cheongsam (a Chinese dress), with a matching coat made overnight. The work on these items was beautiful perfection.

Then it was again a week that quickly passed. We had made many friends. Many of them came with us to the dock to board the SS Victoria, an Italian ship. They had brought their scarves with them and waved them to us as we were on the ship. We saw them for quite a distance as we sailed away from the dock.

The SS Victoria was a beautiful, massive ship. We were in the middle of the ship, about the third floor down. During our travel across the Indian ocean, we had a lot of turbulence. Our ship would stand almost straight up in the air a couple of times. Many people got seasick and couldn't enjoy the voyage, but Reta and I had no such troubles. We said that all our hard life in New Guinea, living amongst the dirt, diseases, and unsanitary conditions, visiting New Guineans in their homes, etc. made us strong. We never got sick for the whole trip. God was taking good care of us. Reta and I settled into our room, it had a bunk bed, close quarters, but we weren't in the cabin too much. There was so much entertainment on the ship.

The ship was very elegant. The dining room was beautiful, with white table cloths and napkins, centerpieces of the area's designs, vases of flowers, animal sculptures, etc. We always dressed formally for dinner and were seated at our table. A napkin was placed on our lap, and any kind of drink we wished for was served. Excellent fish, lamb, beef, chicken, and pork dinners were served. The desserts were delicious! Pavlovas, cakes, ice cream of any flavor, parfaits, and fruits of any kind were available to us.

Our first stop was Singapore. We got there about 4:00 PM and would leave the next morning, so we got off the ship and walked the streets to see all we could. We bought some items at the many markets. We even ate some food at the food stand. It was spicy but delicious. We figured since it was cooked, we should be okay, and we were. Then on to Calcutta.

While on the ship, we had planned entertainment, dances, charades, plays, movies, etc. This helped us to get to know people on the boat of many different nationalities. People were so friendly and fun-loving. We met Phyllis and Barbara, who had been missionaries in Japan. We also met a gal from England, Elizabeth, a missionary. We always went out together when we got into a port, mostly for safety.

Calcutta was very poor. There were cows on the street (cows are considered sacred in India) and people lying in the streets begging for food and money. We did go to the market and bought some beautiful lace doilies, a blouse, and metal vases. Then back on the ship and on to Colombo, Sri Lanka.

We walked the streets of Sri Lanka. It was very poor there, with people on the streets begging and cows loose in the street. We had lunch at a nice-looking restaurant. We ordered rice with spicy beans and condiments. Then onto Bombay, another impoverished area; people begging on dusty streets. We went into a clinic with many sick people. More prosperous people lived in better housing with fenced-in yards. We ate at a nice restaurant; had rice and vegetables with about ten condiments. The dishes were all very hot with lots of spices, especially curry. Then on to Karachi.

We had two days in Karachi, so we saw a little more. There was a beautiful American embassy covered in gold plate there.

We also went to worship at an Episcopal Church, a beautiful cathedral, for their Even Song service. Again, we loved the markets with their beautiful wares. I bought a beautiful silk blouse there for only fifty cents.

Life on the ship was also beautiful because we saw a lot of activity in the Indian Ocean: porpoises bouncing in and out of the water; other sea creatures bouncing up and down; the blue water, high waves; and most gorgeous sunsets. Our next stop was Aden on the Coast of Yemen.

I had developed a terrible toothache, so I said to Reta, "We need to find a dentist." We walked the streets and found a dentist in a shoddy looking building; it was not very clean. We went up the stairs and into the office. It was not sanitary, so Reta said, "You are not going to have anything done here." So, we went down to the street and found a nicer looking restaurant and had lunch. A nice-looking lady walked in with a military uniform. I went up to her and asked if she knew a dentist. She said, "Oh Honey, you come with me to our Air Force base; we'll take care of you." We went to the British Royal Air Force Base and were treated royally! They pulled my tooth, and I was fine.

Then we sailed on to Suez. We got off the ship and onto buses for a Cairo tour while the ship went through the Suez Canal. What a lot of Egypt we got to see! The Nile River, the Egyptian Museum, the streets of Cairo, and a camel ride to the pyramids, as well as a tour into the pyramid where a pharaoh was buried. His tomb was filled with all the tools, food, jewels, and other items he had been buried with. We enjoyed the camel ride back to Cairo to our bus.

The bus then took us to Port Said to meet our ship again. We were to fly to Israel for a tour of Jerusalem, but this did not happen. Israel was at war, and we couldn't go in. We were sad we couldn't go to Israel but hoped we'd get there someday. Then we sailed across the beautiful Mediterranean Sea to Naples, Italy.

We disembarked the ship except for our suitcases, which we had sent on to London to be in storage until we got on the Queen Elizabeth. We, first of all, looked for a youth hostel for the night. Then we toured the city. We kept only a small carry bag with us with rayon sheets, two changes of clothes, and a few toiletries. We also carried a purse on our arm. We should have had a backpack, but we didn't know about them in those days.

In Naples, we saw the city and had an Italian meal, pizza with a lot of olive oil. Italy is known for beautiful shoes, so we each bought a pair of pumps with high heels which we thought we could squeeze in our carrying bags. We then had our first hitch-hiking experience. At the youth hostel, we met young people who gave us a lot of traveling information. We quickly got a ride to Rome. We always found a youth hostel first thing.

Rome is a beautiful city on seven hills. We took in the sights: St. Peter Cathedral, The Colosseum, and Three Fountains where we dropped in our money, as was the custom, and made our wish! We climbed the Prayer Steps on our knees. We enjoyed the friendly, loving people. We looked like vagabonds, so no one ever thought we were American/Canadian.

Then we got a ride to Pompei to see Mount Vesuvius and walked through the city's ruins. We couldn't believe how much excavation had been done. Many everyday living items all around, even houses with courtyards, were excavated so we could imagine their lives before the volcano.

Our next ride took us to Florence. A retired policeman picked us up. We had such a fun ride; he was very jovial. We kept learning words in Italian from him. We'd point to something, and he'd say the Italian word, like "uva" for grapes. It was a beautiful city.

We especially enjoyed the big church and baptistry attached to it. The paintings and artwork on the walls were something to behold—beautiful pictures of Jesus and his disciples, Bible stories, creation, etc.

Then on to Pisa to see the leaning tower. We got a ride with three young boys in a Volkswagen. They were a lot of fun, and we tried to speak via sign language. When we got to Pisa, they kept following us, so we climbed the tower and had a hide and seek adventure. When we got down, we thumbed for another ride back to Florence and got rid of the young men!

At Florence, we caught a ride to Venice. It was such an exciting city. We rode the gondolas through the canals and saw people had their clothes hanging out on poles to dry. We stopped at St. Mark's square and fought our way through the pigeons and crowd of people. The cathedral again was beautiful with paintings and carvings. At the market, we bought a little gondola and paddle and pictures. We each had a camera and were taking our own pictures also. Then we got a ride to Milan, another beautiful city. We enjoyed the large opera house and an evening at the opera, "Die Fledermaus."

On to Zurich, Switzerland. What a beautiful clean country. We had a wonderful roast beef meal, took a gondola up into the mountains, saw cows with cowbells, beautiful chateaus, green pastures, and paddocks. Men wore lederhosen and blew long horns; it was all so beautiful. They spoke German, so I could communicate some. We also saw the building where the Lord's Supper is painted on the wall. It was heavily guarded.

We then took a ride across the mountains to Heidelberg. We walked the beautiful walkways along the river, trees in full fall colors. We were now in Germany. Since I knew "low German," it was easier to carry on a conversation. We visited a museum and markets with many beautiful creations, dishes, fruits and vegetables, clothing, and fresh flowers. Reta and I bought a kilo of grapes and a kilo of cheese for our meals as we had little money.

At the youth hostels, we could buy Coke bottles filled with weak wine for five cents, an alternative to water, which was not safe to drink. We could get a continental breakfast at the youth hostel. We paid fifty cents a night to stay at the hostels, using our own sheets and towels. In Germany, we sometimes stayed at a pensione. They were inexpensive; we got a good bed, an evening meal, and a continental breakfast. From Heidelberg, we took a boat trip up the Rhine River to Cologne. The scenery on both sides of the river was magnificent, with beautiful castles dotting the mountains on the river's east side.

In Cologne, we saw a cathedral that was destroyed in World War II. It was being repaired beautifully. We did a lot of sightseeing around the area. Everyone seemed to keep their homes cared for beautifully. We saw the Berlin Wall. We took a taxi down the Autobahn to get there. It was a sad sight and to think the people on the other side had no freedom.

From there, we got a ride to Luxembourg. It was a beautiful clean country. Houses and barns were cared for beautifully. We even got to see a parade: Queen Juliana was in a carriage at the parade's beginning. She waved at all of us and was beautifully dressed in a crown of beautiful stones and a suit made of silk. We loved Luxembourg.

On to Paris where again we found a bustling and crowded city. The people were a little snobbish, but Reta could speak French, so we did well. We toured the Notre Dame Cathedral, and it was so beautiful. The altar area lifted you up as you saw murals and statutes of Jesus, the apostles, and angels everywhere. We walked along the Seine River, and many artists were at work with their canvasses. Some of the productions were beautiful, and we wished we had money to buy one. We toured the Louvre for a day, but we wished we had more time. So many paintings and statues. Like the one of King David from the Bible, the Mona Lisa, and so much more. It was breathtaking! We climbed the Eifel Tower and went through the Arch of Triumphe Gate. From the tower, you have a good view of Paris. We visited the Cathedral of St. Louis, and it was awesome, then we went downstairs to see the crypt of Louis the Fourteenth. Before you could get in, you had to wait in line, and there were some chairs along the side, so we sat down to wait.

When we finally went upstairs, I realized I didn't have my purse. This was a scare as it had my passport, money, and American Express card, so I panicked. Reta said, "I'll go up to the door and watch the people that leave; you look through the cathedral." I looked around the main floor and saw nothing. Then I went back down where the crypt was, and there under the chair where I had sat was my purse. My heart jumped for joy, and I thanked and praised God all day and for days after.

We then got a ride to Versailles and toured the beautiful hall. Again, it awed us as the ceiling paintings, walls, and chandeliers were just so beautiful. It took a whole day to see it all.

Then we were on to Brussels, Belgium. It was a unique city with a famous square where people go for walking, information about the latest happenings in government, and social occasions. They have a statue of a little boy peeing into a basin. It was a famous place as people took pictures in front of it.

On to Holland. Amsterdam was our first stop, and of course, it was a busy city. We liked the way people dressed in their bonnets, full dresses, and simple, well-built shoes. We visited the home of Anne Frank, and it was sad. We saw where the family hid upstairs and the entrance behind a bookcase. The anxiety they lived through was terrible, living in fear they could be found at any time. They were Jews hiding from the Nazis who killed all Jews if found. The family that hid Anne Frank's family was also in great danger. I was glad I had read "The Diary of Anne Frank" as all that we saw and heard made the book come alive. We walked the streets and took a tour of the Prinsengracht Canal, from which we saw beautiful Dutch Row Houses. They were clean and ornate.

Then we got a ride to Volendam and Millendam, and what a quaint and unique place. The houses were row houses, all with peaked roofs and one door to enter the house. Outside on a little porch were wooden shoes. Beautiful lace curtains were at the windows. Inside was an entry room, kitchen, and dining room joined. All the furniture was made of wood. Upstairs were the bedrooms, but we didn't get up there. Wood stoves were used for cooking. We had a bus tour of the tulip fields; they were beautiful – just a mass of color. The people were so friendly and loving. Of course, I had to buy a pair of wooden shoes that I still treasure. I bought a miniature pair for each of my nieces and nephews as a gift.

We did not get to Normandy; our hearts were sad to think of all the boys in World War II who so tragically lost their lives to save Europe and the U.S. Then we crossed the English Channel on a small ship.

There were loudspeakers on the ship telling the many things that had happened on the channel. People swam across the English Channel throughout history. We couldn't believe it as it is quite a distance across the channel. We remembered the conflicts over the channel in World War II and thanked God that war came to a peaceful end, but only after many lives were lost.

Then our arrival in London! What an exciting city. We stayed with our friend Elizabeth who we got to know well on the ship. We had a lot of tea, scones, and biscuits (cookies). We walked around the city and rode on the double-decker buses. We enjoyed visiting Trafalgar Square with the Lord Nelson statue in the middle. He was a war hero in England.

We went to Buckingham Palace and saw the changing of the guard. It was so impressive; the process was done with such precision. We also got to see Queen Elizabeth in a carriage – it was like a parade – taking her to the Parliament House.

We went to the Tower of London where the crown jewels are kept. We toured there and were in great awe of the many crowns of jewels. There were many other beautiful displays of gems and treasures to see. On Sunday evening, we went to St. Paul's Cathedral for the Even Song service. It was beautiful. The message was very biblical, and the choirs sounded heavenly. Reta and I were happy when we could take in a service, which helped our spirits rejoice.

We also visited Westminster Abbey, where many kings, queens, and influential people are buried. Again, it was stunning inside with stained windows, decorated ceilings so high they lifted you heavenward, and awe-inspiring paintings and statutes.

Then I was able to go to Wales to visit friends, Reverend Marvin and Hildegard Brammeier, and their family. Reta stayed in London and did a tour of the countryside.

The Brammeier's took me on a tour of Cardiff, an interesting place, a lot of influence from the sea. We went through a mine where they dug slate, which is now obsolete but was used a lot in buildings and roads. Marvin and Hildegard went to England as missionaries and had a congregation of about one hundred and fifty members and growing. We talked about missions often as we were all so involved in it.

After I got back, Reta and I took a tour to see the White Cliffs of Dover. The walls were unbelievable, all of white stone. Then it was time to go to the docks where our ship, Queen Elizabeth II, was waiting for us. We were so thankful to see our luggage being loaded and that it had arrived safely from Naples. The ship was beautiful. We kept thanking God for all these wonderful privileges He was letting us experience.

The Queen Elizabeth II had a beautiful interior with an elaborate dining room, similar to the SS Victoria. Formal dress was again the norm for dinner. The exclusively male waiters were exceptional. The food was so delicious, dishes of food with exotic names. We were treated like queens. The waiter would seat us, put the napkin on our lap, and ask us to pick from many drinks: coffee, tea, juices of various kinds, many types of wines, etc. The evening entertainment was delightful with music concerts, movies, charades, dancing, and other activities. People were so friendly; it was always easy to strike up a conversation.

The ride across the ocean was very calm. As we drew near to New York, we were getting so excited. We had traveled across the Orient, often saying, "This is like America!". When we visited Europe and England, each seemed more American until we landed in New York City. Nothing could equal it; it was just so beautiful. We rejoiced that we had such a beautiful, wonderful country. I guess we had forgotten a little being in New Guinea for three years.

Forty-five members from the church at Levittown were there to greet us as we got off the ship. They had supported me while I taught in their school and had taken care of my needs in New Guinea. Here they were again. What a reunion! We hugged and kissed; it was just beyond words. They had reserved a room at a lovely restaurant, and we all ate lunch together.

It was just such an emotional meal; the conversations varied from our trip, life in New Guinea, to them catching us up on the U.S. After the meal, Reta and I had a hard time saying goodbye. She was taking a train to Kitchener, Ontario, Canada, her home.

I went to Levittown for five days and did many lecture evenings on New Guinea at four churches, during the day visiting. It was a surreal week – so much joy. Then my sister Wilma and brother Luther arrived from Illinois to drive me home. My parents were delighted to see me. My family and many friends were excited that I had returned home. The churches around Southern Illinois who all had supported me were glad to have me back. I enjoyed my lectures in Illinois and had some in other congregations who supported me with prayers and donations from Iowa, Kansas, Missouri, Indiana, and Michigan. I shared my view of New Guinea and all that my wonderful Lord Jesus let me do and see.

Then I had to decide what was next. I had six months of furlough, but I knew I needed more, so I asked for a year. This meant I needed to find work for six months. From December 1962 to June 1963, I was able to get a teaching job at Bethesda Lutheran School in Jennings, Missouri. They were remodeling their school, so we had classes in the basement of the police department. Mr. Herbert Schollmeyer was the principal. I had grades one through four, and he had grades five through eight. It was different once again – any material I needed for my classroom was at my fingertips. I just made a trip to the store and bought it. We were in a very secure location, so no worries. The policemen were very kind, and I had them give two presentations to my students. I enjoyed my six months there.

Dad helped me buy a Volkswagen, coral color, and I really enjoyed it. A congregation member who lived close to the police department let me live in their finished basement. I also worked with the church's youth. One day, I was walking down the street with one of these youths, Eileen Sims, and my brother Luther came along. He worked at Lambert Airport, so he often stopped in to see me. He later dated Eileen, and they were married.

In July, I reported to the Mission Board in St. Louis, Missouri, and told them I was ready for another term in New Guinea. I did some more lectures in the summer and visited with friends and family until I was prepared to leave.

One of those weekends, Janet Priebe, Judy McCormick, and Marjorie Ellman visited me. They had been in Kentucky for midwifery training and were leaving for New Guinea a week later. Having firsthand knowledge of New Guinea helped them, and we worked together in New Guinea for many years.

In August of 1963, I again boarded TWA to California then took Pan Am across the Pacific Ocean. It was easy this time; I knew where I was going. I stopped in San Francisco and was met by Betty and Dave Raff and some of the other LWML women. They had collected some of the items I would need and were sending them to New Guinea. To have a bond in Jesus like I had with these women and everyone I had contact with on furlough was such a spirit-lifting experience. Again, "The love of Jesus, what it is, none but His loved ones know."

Once again, the Pan Am ride to Hawaii, Fiji, and Sydney was beautiful and smooth. We got a large poster every time we crossed the International Date Line. The plane rides were long but enjoyable; the stewards and stewardesses treated us with royal service.

When I got to Sydney, there were more flights to New Guinea than on my first trip. I stayed with my friends, the Nelsons, for two days and did some shopping in Sydney. I liked their David Jones department stores.

On the flight to Port Moresby, one of the engines on the plane stopped. We had to make an emergency stop in Townsville, Australia. I was sitting by the window when the engine stopped and saw the problem. I panicked a little. Soon the captain's voice came over the intercom and assured us we'd be okay until we landed in Townsville.

I spent three days in Townsville and got acquainted with the city and more of the Australian way of life and their way of speaking English. They have an accent that is a little hard to understand at first. Some of the other passengers, three couples going to our mission, walked around the city with me. This being the tropics, we had our share of pineapple, mangoes, breadfruit, oranges, grapefruit, and whatever else they had.

On the third day, we flew on to Port Moresby, Papua New Guinea and again the DC-3 to Mt. Hagen, then on to Wapenamanda.

CHAPTER 11

Back in New Guinea

A group of workers from the business office came to meet me, and we had a family reunion. They drove me up to Yaibos, and I had a reunion with the Kleinig family and others working on that station. Then I went to Pausa to my little house which was waiting for me. I got a few pieces of furniture back from missionaries on the station. I got a bed and food from the business office and got settled quickly.

On September 1st, 1963, I taught again at St Paul's Lutheran High School at Pausa, where I had worked before. It was a joy to be back and work in New Guinea! I was working with different staff at St. Paul's Lutheran High School. The previous staff had left on furlough or ended their term.

Life was good. We had many more girls attending, and I was always taking special care of them, dealing with their social and emotional needs in addition to their educational needs. They proved to be outstanding students, excelling in Math, English, Social Studies, and learning to care for people by working at the hospital. To see our students excelling in their studies was so rewarding. Many went on to work as nurses in training, secretaries in the banking industry, teachers, or started businesses of their own. This all brought great joy to us teachers because we knew the poor primitive conditions they came from were not hindering their initiative!

I wrote a Christmas pageant (The Christmas Story) and got a group of students to do the parts: Mary, Joseph, Baby Jesus, angel, shepherds, wisemen. We made a barn out of tar paper, and it was attached to wooden poles, built a wooden manger, and made bales out of tall grass. There was no problem getting help because this was exciting for the students. Vivian Bauer and Joyce Lehman helped make the costumes. We could buy cheap material brought in from Hong Kong. We took the play to several mission stations and performed. It was a great mission project, and the story of Jesus' birth was confirmed in many minds and hearts.

Performing at the New Guinea churches was a challenge as they were large bush buildings, and acoustics were not good, but we always had a quiet audience.

The students accompanied me to many outstations on Sunday morning to teach Sunday School. It was a one or two-hour walk over mountain paths and bridges, which were just poles. The kids were very experienced in walking over these, so they held both of my hands firmly. We were on the Lord's mission, so He kept us safe. Sometimes the stations were further away. We would leave on Saturday afternoon and stay the night, then attend church on Sunday morning and walk back home. We slept in their homes, which were usually flea-infested, but we didn't let that bother us. We had brought anti-itch medication with us. We ate their sweet potato cooked in a pit with wood in their bush home. Often on Sunday, they would get up early and kill some chickens and put them with sweet potato in a hole lined with banana leaves, and they would heat stones and put them in the hole before they put the banana leaves in, then cover it with dirt. After Sunday School lessons and the church service and about 5 hours of cooking, we would have a delicious lunch. Then we would say our goodbyes and go on our walk home. The love these people showed us was inspiring; they never wanted us to leave.

One of our Form I Classes (Grades 1 and 2)

Some of our students November 1970
St. Paul's Lutheran, Wapenamanda, New Guinea. Up until 1970 it was known
only as Pausa Lutheran School

Outdoor worship service, January 30, 1963, at Yaibos. The officiant Waiema Waesa, near the van. Worship was held outdoors prior to a church being built.

Eunice wrote a Christmas Pagent and the students presented it at all the churches in the Lai Valley. They loved it.

Chapter 12

Agricultural and Economic Progress

We had passed out vegetable seeds to the people by this time, and they were growing potatoes, carrots, beans, radishes, and other plants for themselves to improve their diet. They would also bring some of their extra produce to our station, and we would buy them. At first, money meant nothing to them as they had nowhere to spend it, so we bartered with salt, matches, sugar, pocketknives: things they could use. After a while, the mission started little trade stores at each station where we sold all the items listed plus other items they could use. Thus, money became something they learned to use, so we could even pay them when they did work for us. We trained boys to clean our houses, cut firewood for our stoves, and wash our clothes. The clothes washing was done by rubbing the laundry on a board in a tub of water, rinsing the clothes, and hanging them on a wire between two poles. Our teaching kept us very busy, so having the boys clean was very helpful. They were so happy to earn a little money to spend at the small trade store. More and more things were being put in the trade stores, so it broadened their horizons.

Students in the garden at St. Paul's Lutheran High School
harvesting their own food.

CHAPTER 13

Climb up Mt. Hagen

During my second term, one of the highlight adventures was a climb up Mt. Hagen, a 14,000-foot-high mountain. The foot of this mountain was about ten miles down the road from Pausa. Anita Simonson, a nurse; Althea Weier, secretary; and I, decided we'd like to climb the mountain. We were told by the Kiaps, government police, that this would not be a good idea, but we decided to give it a try anyway.

Our stations were at 6,000 feet, so it would be a steep climb. So, we prepared for the trip. We got eight schoolboys to go with us to carry our food and gear. The morning we were ready to leave, Kondenk, the elder from Yaramonda, our congregation near Pausa, was waiting for us at the mountain's foot. There were several men with him. They felt we girls needed protection. The food we took was cans of sweetened condensed milk, cans of Spaghetti-O's, homemade bread and butter. The men brought sweet potatoes and sugar cane.

We climbed up the mountain. It was steep! We made stops to eat sugar cane and drink sweetened condensed milk. It was best to keep up our energy level. About six in the evening, we got to the flat area below the summit. We decided to camp there and then climb to the summit the next morning. So, the boys put up our tar paper tent. They had brought five poles to brace it. We just walked around and looked and looked. The view was so spectacular. We were fortunate to be there on very clear days. Then we ate our Spaghetti-O's and bread and, oh yes, cookies we had brought. It was a feast. We shared with the boys and men and had such a fun evening. Then at dusk, we settled into our sleeping bags in our tent. The boys had blankets and settled at the foot of our tent. It got very cold during the night, and we started feeling bodies moving closer around our feet in the tent. Well, it brought more warmth into the tent! We did sleep and woke up at about five the next morning.

We got up. The morning greeted us with a glorious view! It was a beautiful clear day, and we could see for miles. We ate some bread and biscuits (cookies) and started our climb to the summit. Well, it was breathtaking – the view was magnificent. When we reached the summit, we could see all around us. We could even see Mt. Wilhelm, the highest mountain in the distance. We sang "Praise God from Whom All Blessings Flow" and said prayers of thanks to the Lord for letting us see this wonder of His creation. We were there for at least three hours with great elation.

We descended to our camping spot where we had left the tent behind, but had taken our other gear with us. Thank God for our boys, our carriers! The descent was much faster and easier. We did stop to rejuvenate with sweetened condensed milk and sugar cane. We had to stop occasionally just to enjoy the view. When we got to the bottom, several jeeps were waiting, driven by mission staff, to take us back to Pausa. Thank God, we climbed the mountain and for the great joy that brought us! The memories are forever in our minds.

*Althea, Eunice, and Anita on top of Mt. Hagen, 14,000 feet.
Quite a climb but a fun and good one!*

*Seeing the top of Mt. Wihelm from the top of Mt. Hagen. Mt. Wihelm is the
highest in Papua New Guinea.*

CHAPTER 14

Back to America

In the middle of my second term, my father became very ill. I decided to go home during our school summer break (December 15, 1964 through January 13, 1965) to see my parents. Once again, I took a long flight across the ocean. The Australian airline Qantas was comfortable. The stewards and stewardesses were very kind and helpful, making it a very smooth trip. My friends, Betty and Dave Raff, met me in San Francisco, and spending a night with them was a spiritual renewal.

Then on to St. Louis and home. I had four weeks with my parents. It was spent reminiscing, visiting relatives, and giving several lectures on New Guinea at churches who supported me in the area. My father had cancer. When I left, I knew I would not see him in this world again. We were comforted with Bible readings and the assurance of a grand reunion in heaven.

CHAPTER 15

Return to New Guinea

Upon return to New Guinea, I settled into school life after the long flight. Teaching my students was a joy. However, I felt some sadness that I was losing my father. During Lent, I went to Mambisanda one Wednesday evening for a Lenten service. The pastor was Rev. James Herzog. His sermon was so comforting and uplifting, so I spoke to him after the Lenten service. He said, "I'll come over to Pausa tomorrow afternoon after school, and we'll get more comfort and help from God's Word." Well, we found such comfort and upbuilding from God's Word that I was so thankful to God for sending him to help me find great help from His Word.

Rev. Herzog came every afternoon for a week – what a friend! What a mentor! He told me I should get up every morning an hour earlier than I had been and pray. "If you run out of prayers," he said, "sit at your typewriter and type some Psalms from the Bible." What comfort and strength I gained and life was not hard anymore. God was my guide and friend, and I got everything I needed from the joy and strength His Word provided. Jim became my lifelong mentor and friend. He had a lovely wife, Betty, and two sons, James Jr. and Sam, who became like family to me.

In May, my father went to his heavenly home, and I was sad but also strengthened and comforted by God's word and by Jim and his family, plus many others of our mission family. I realized how blessed I was to have all these God-fearing people to work with, plus all the people who had heard God's word and were witnesses to me, especially many of our students. No words can describe the beautiful life God gives us when we give ourselves to Him and let Him lead and guide us and strengthen us in faith through His Word.

CHAPTER 16
Life Moves On

The following July, we had our missionary conference at Amapyaka, where our mission children went to school. They would be on break, and the mission staff would take over the place. We used the dorms for sleeping and a large room in the administration, music, and classroom building for our meetings. Our conferences were very spiritually rich. Pastors had wonderful devotions each day, and we had an inspiring worship service with communion at the beginning and end of each meeting. They always got pastors or professors from Australia and the U.S. as guest speakers. During the conference, we would often break out in beautiful hymns. Usually, we had enough business to be there for four or five days. Since I was a teacher and the only organist, I was included and played the music. Well, the pastors and teachers sang with such gusto it was a joy to play for them.

At one particular conference, our speaker was Dr. Alfred Rehwinkel from the U.S., a professor at our Concordia Seminary in St. Louis. He had written a book called "The Flood." He lectured on that book and the flood of Noah's time in the Bible and spoke on chapters in other parts of the Bible.

On the plane that brought Dr. Rehwinkel to the highlands was a young man from Australia, Ray Hausler. He was called to

New Guinea as a carpenter in the field. He was an accomplished builder, having completed his apprenticeship. Es and Clem Janetzki, who were letting him board at their house, introduced him to the conference. He looked so young. I knew he would fit in with the other young Australian men on our staff.

About three weeks after the conference, the Hagen Show would be held at Mt. Hagen. This was a show where many of the Highland tribes came to show off their dances, get to know each other, admire each other's dress, and became acquainted with each other's ways of life.

Es and Clem Janetzki and Henry and Elsie Weier, an older carpenter couple, were taking some students and as many New Guineans as possible to Mt. Hagen. They would take as many people as the truck would hold and would transport the missionary students to Mt. Hagen to catch a flight to Port Moresby and then on to Melbourne, Australia, where these missionary children went to high school.

It was always hard to see the missionary children spend so much time away from their homes while they furthered their education.

My friend Dawn Jericho and I decided to go with the Janetzkes and Weiers to the Hagen show. This was in August of 1965. The morning they came by Pausa on the way to Mt. Hagen, my friend Dawn didn't arrive with them. They said she was sick. I hesitated going, but I knew I might never see the show unless I went, so I did. It was a bumpy but fun ride as we kept cheering up the children knowing they were sad to leave home again for school. The Janetzki's brought along their new boarder, Ray Hausler. When we got to Mt. Hagen, we took the children to the airport and saw them get on the plane, an emotional moment. Then we went to the show.

So, we started walking around at the show. Mr. and Mrs. Weier went together, Clem and Es Janetzki went together, leaving this Ray fellow and myself together. We followed the Janetzke's and the Weier's. The show was very interesting and educational.

We learned a lot about the various tribes of the Highlands. Their dress was different, a lot of colors. Men wore belts with Tonka leaves and colorful paint on their faces and big black hats made of hair on their heads. Each tribe was different. One tribe covered themselves with mud and then put on the belts, leaves, paint, and hats. The women wore grass skirts, no blouses – bare chests, painted faces, and carried billums on their head (bags made of string made from the hemp plant). Ray and I did a little getting acquainted with conversation during the day.

That evening we went to a shed filled with coffee beans. Several other young men from our mission who had attended the show met us there. We decided the women would sleep on the back of the Land Rover, and the men would sleep on the coffee beans. That evening the four young men and I went to the restaurant/bar for a little entertainment. This Ray Hausler was getting more and more friendly. He looked and seemed so young that I really didn't think of our relationship as more than him being just another worker on the field. On the ride home, Ray sat next to me in the back of the truck with Mr. Weier and about fifteen New Guineans. He talked a lot on the way back to Pausa.

We got home and back to our usual routine and work. One afternoon Ray came over after work from Yaibos for a visit. I was a little surprised, but we talked a lot. He was a very Christian man, and we talked a lot about God in our lives. Ray had been trained in a Lutheran College in Toowoomba, Australia, and had wanted to be a pastor but learning Greek and Hebrew was difficult. Instead, he went into the construction trade and got a degree as a journeyman. Ray was a good builder. He made some beautiful altars, lecterns, and pulpits for three churches in Redcliffe and Toowoomba, Australia, which he shared with me. But to get into a serious relationship was a challenge for me. I had dated fine Christian men, but being a missionary-teacher was my life now, and I was happy.

Ray came to visit me more and more, and I prayed a lot. Did I really want to get serious and change my profession? Well, I had asked the mission to let me teach at an outstation, where we had started schools that had become coeducational. So, I was told I could do so at Sirunki, a station at a higher elevation, more isolated of course; this is what I wanted, so in January of 1966, I moved up to Sirunki. By then, Ray and I had gotten very friendly. He would have to ride the motorbike 45 miles on rough roads up to Sirunki to visit me. An excellent way to find out if someone really loves you!

CHAPTER 17

Christmas and a Proposal

In December 1965, we single people decided to fly out to Mara-muni, a station only reachable by air. Rev Wagner had to get watch boys every time a plane flew in as pigs ran across the airstrip, which was hazardous. One aircraft was damaged and almost crashed, so those boys were essential.

Rev. Merlin and Jan Wagner were stationed there and were terrific hosts. We had a fantastic four days; everybody helped cook, planned evenings of games, told stories and worshipped with the New Guineans. What a beautiful Christmas service we had. We helped them put up a manger surrounded with wooden figures: Mary, Joseph, Baby Jesus, the shepherds, and Wisemen. We all grew in faith and joy. Ray came to Sirunki with us as he was doing some carpentry work there.

The first evening we were back, Ray came over. He kind of overwhelmed me as he asked me to marry him. I thought about it, and he seemed like someone I would like to spend my life with, so I gave my consent.

The church at Maramuni where the single staff went for Christmas one year. Guards kept the pigs off the airstrip.

CHAPTER 18

Life at Sirunki

Dick and Loretta Adler lived at Sirunki. He taught standards (grades) six through eight, and I had standards one through four. We also had Rev. William Wagner and his wife, Ruth, there. I settled in quite quickly.

Teaching thirty-four young children was a real joy. They were quick learners. The school was a bush building with row benches and desks, not the best arrangement, but we made it work. You do a lot of creating posters, wall hangings, visual aids, all made by hand when you can't go to the store to buy them.

We had an electric generator on our station to be used only at night until ten PM. One evening I wanted to use my clothes iron and plugged it in. The generator revved up and scared me. Soon Dick Adler was at my door, wondering what I was doing. Well, I was embarrassed, but hey, you have to try and see what you can do!

At the end of May, the Wagner's left on furlough, and then in July, the Adler's went to work in Madang. I was left at the station alone. I was not afraid as the New Guineans were my family. I learned later the elders took turns sleeping on a ridge below my house to make sure I wasn't harmed. After Adlers left,

I moved into their house. It was a more permanent house with wood-framed walls covered with Masonite siding. It was a luxury and even had an indoor toilet and bathroom!

Being the only one on the station, I had to take care of the sick as well. I had learned how to give shots for influenza, which I did several times. One evening they brought a lady in, badly burned. I took care of her as best I could and called out to the next station for a jeep to take her to Mambisanda, a forty-mile run down the valley to the mission hospital. I rode with her. It was a long night with the ride down, and she was suffering terribly, but she got good treatment once we got her to the hospital. I was pretty shook-up seeing her suffer so. She came back a month later healed.

Eunice's school class at Sirunki. They also sang at Eunice and Ray's wedding. Every morning they sang, "God Save the Queen."

CHAPTER 19

Wedding Plans

In July, I started planning our wedding. Ray and I were going to be married on November 26th, 1966, at Amapyaka, where our mission students went to school. We would fix up one of the larger rooms to look like a church, and it would hold a large crowd.

The congregation at Levittown, especially the ladies, got on board. They had a bridal shower for me and sent about everything I needed for a wedding. One of my students at Levittown, Candace Werberig, was grown now. She was my size, so they used her as a model to make my dress. The dress was made of white Chinese brocade; it was gorgeous and fit perfectly. They included a veil, shoes, and all the accessories.

I wanted my thirty-two students to sing at our wedding. Nancy Kunert, friend and teacher's wife, came up one weekend, and we sewed thirty-two gowns with aqua sashes. We used the white lap lap material from Hong Kong. Ray and his best man and groomsman ordered suits from Hong Kong. They were black and made with excellence. They ordered shoes and white shirts as well. Dick Adler was Best Man; Garry Wolf was groomsman. They were three sharp looking men!

We also needed a cake. In Australia, fruit cake is the celebration cake. Elinor Burce, Dr. Burce's wife, said she would make it. It was a major task. She baked four layers of fruit cake in graduating sizes. She baked them in August and then wrapped them in cloth and soaked them in brandy until November. In November, the week before the wedding, she started the icing. It was a hefty first layer of icing, then a heavy, smooth layer of marzipan over that.

Each layer had a theme. The lower layer was covered with bells made of sugar for the "Joy of Christian Marriage." The next layer was covered with grains, all handmade, for fertility in our marriage. The third layer was the fruit of the vine, grapes, and leaves, for "Fruitfulness and Happiness." The top layer was a silver cross, a Chi-Rho with double rings at the cross-section, for "Marriage in Christ." The decoration around the layers was so beautiful, with swirls and puffed lines. Ray made heavy rods to hold each layer, and each layer was on a metal plate covered with several layers of white butcher paper. It was about thirty-six inches tall. There were many "ohs" and "ahs" when the people saw it.

My friend and bridesmaid was Janice Haby, a secretary from Australia. Loretta Adler was the maid of honor. They gave me a bridal shower at Amapyaka in October. Most of our missionary ladies were able to make it. Any party was always a fun occasion in New Guinea. With the gifts from my New Guinea shower and the shower the ladies in Levittown gave me, Ray and I had many of the things we needed for our home.

I finished the school year at Sirunki with joy. I had thirty-two children that had learned so much and were so courteous and respectful. We had a big party on the last day of school, and the parents cooked food, a muum pit in the ground with hot stones in the hole covered with banana leaves, then some chicken, and a pig was killed for the occasion, topped with sweet potatoes and cooked from 6:00 AM till 12:00 PM.

Parents and children were all excited. We had our religion lesson, memory work, and then played games. They loved playing circle games as well as hide-and-go-seek and the wolf game – counting to twelve and then looking for the wolf and hoping you could run faster than he/she back to the base. Then we ate our dinner, and they all enjoyed the food; nothing was left. We sang secular songs, hymns and closed with prayers. I told the students that I had gotten a truck to get them the day before the wedding and wanted them to sing for us. Great excitement arose in the crowd.

On November 19th, I moved down to Amapyaka to stay with the Adler's to get ready for the wedding. We fixed up the large schoolroom by hanging white drapes made of cloth across the front where the altar was put. The school had a large cross, which we put above the altar. They filled the room with all the chairs they could muster up.

Ray, with his boys, built a large tent area. They covered the area with white cloth and set up long tables underneath where the food would sit. The wedding party would sit at another long table. We had a meal catered by Richard and Beth Brandon and Jim and Carol Barton. They made salads, cold cuts, cheese slices, homemade bread, and cut up fruit. The missionary wives also brought cakes and biscuits (cookies). They prepared large containers of tea, lemonade, and water: everybody helped, and all went very smoothly. We had ninety-five missionaries on the field at that time and their families. We knew they would all come as we were a close family. Then we invited my students and Ray's students plus the leaders of the New Guinea Church and government workers in our area. We planned for four hundred people.

November 25th came, and we had a rehearsal with a rehearsal dinner. The Adler's made the rehearsal dinner with candles, and we had turkey and trimmings – you see, it was Thanksgiving time in the U.S. For dessert, they made Baked Alaska, and it was superb. Bill Wagner and his family were there. Rev. Wagner served as the liturgist for the wedding. Rev. Jim Herzog and family came, and Jim was the preacher for the wedding. The evening was so special.

Then came November 26th, 1966, the wedding day! The students arrived the day before and were housed in the homes of leaders of the church at Yaibos. Nancy Kunert took care of them and helped with getting them dressed. She told me later that one boy had missed the truck, and he had walked all night to get there to sing. It upset me. I just thanked God that he was okay.

Janice Haby had ordered Frangipani flowers from the coast for their bouquets. She was up most of the night making those; several other girls helped her. I carried a white prayer book with gardenias hanging from it. The girls had made their own dresses and headpieces from green satin and looked equally lovely. Pastor and Ruth Wagner's daughter, Lisa, was our flower girl. She wore a dress made by the Levittown ladies in white satin. She was about six years old; we became good friends when they were at Sirunki.

We all got dressed at the Adler home. When we walked out to go to the church building, I was overwhelmed. The station was surrounded by New Guineans who all wanted to see the wedding. We had a beautiful sunny morning. The service was at 9 AM because Ray and I had arrangements to fly out on our honeymoon at 12 PM. We knew the clouds would move in after that, and the plane could not fly us out to Goroka.

The service was very special. Reverend Wagner walked me down the aisle in my beautiful Chinese brocade dress. We had a foot pump organ and an accomplished pianist, Marlene Cooper, who played "Trumpet Voluntary," "Sheep May Safely Graze," and "Joyful, Joyful, We Adore Thee" as I walked in. Ray looked so handsome. When I reached the altar, he said, "You are beautiful" to me. That was a very special moment!

Reverend Herzog did such an excellent job of delivering the sermon. Being a special friend and mentor made his sermon very special. His theme was, "Today, a New Mission Station is Being Established." Our hymns were "Take Thou My Hands and Lead Me," "Praise God from Whom All Blessings Flow," "Let Us Ever Walk with Jesus," and the children sang "Children of the Heavenly Father." Our home was to be a "mission station." This was very prophetic as our home has been a mission station during all these succeeding years. Many people have stayed in our house, and many have entered needing help and spiritual encouragement. It's always been a home where Jesus dwells, and He filled it with much love and let us share it with many people.

Anyway, I just enjoyed every minute; it all seemed too overwhelming. I kept saying, "Thank You, Lord, Thank You, Lord! I am not worthy of all the joy and goodness You are giving me!"

We flew out from Goroka to Bulolo, near Lae, where they have a big plywood factory. The people there were so friendly. Finally, I was alone with Ray; it was so good to be together with no one else around. We had a good time.

One afternoon we played lawn bowls, a game of throwing bowling balls at a white ball at the end of the field, it was a memorable afternoon. We got to know about ten couples; I won the game and was given a beautiful plate, cup, and saucer. It seemed so unreal as it was my first time to play.

After three days, we flew on to Menyamya, where Ray's sister and brother-in-law, Russell and Selma Weier, were missionaries. The people there had been cannibals and fierce fighters as they were people of small stature. They were very receptive to the Gospel message and accepted Jesus as their Savior. We enjoyed the worship services so much.

The road into the Menyamya mission station was very muddy, and we had to cross some very shaky bridges. Ray and I enjoyed getting to know each other more and realized we had a lot in common because our childhood lives were very similar. We both grew up on a farm and had wonderful Christian parents who raised us in the fear and admonition of the Lord. Going to church was a regular, every Sunday affair. The Lutheran Church of Australia had the same hymnbooks and liturgy as the LCMS in the U.S. Since I had worked with the Australians for six years, I was accustomed to many of their ways of life: their accents and the different words they use for certain things. Like nursing a baby is "holding a baby," not feeding it; napkins are "serviettes," a baby bed is a "humidicrib," and some other phrases. They have a lot of slang I had learned by hearing them speak.

Eunice and Ray's wedding party November 26, 1966, Amapyaka, New Guinea

Eunice and Ray's wedding cake, a fruit cake, made by Elinor Burce, wife of first missionary to the Western Highlands New Guinea. It took four months to prepare, it soaked in brandy for three months, then covered with two icings, one was marzipan.

Some of the people at their wedding November 26, 1966

Choir at their wedding, Eunice's students from Sirunki. They sang "Children of the Heavenly Father" beautifully and were directed by Nancy Kunert.

CHAPTER 20

Our First Home

After a week at Menyamya, it was time to get back to Pausa and settle into our bush home. It had a separate kitchen because of the wood stove that could be a fire hazard. We also had to get ready for our school year, which always went from February through November.

Ray invited his roommates from the year before to visit us for dinner about our second week home. Well, getting the house in order took a little doing, and I had gotten a box of spices from Betty and Dave Raff in California for our home. I needed a spice rack. Ray was a good carpenter, so I asked him to make me a spice rack. Just a simple one, but he never came forth with one. On the day before the dinner, I got a little upset about the spice rack. He left the house for his school shop. I thought, "Oh my, I've upset him now! In a little while, I saw him coming down the road with a beautiful spice rack. He had made it for a Christmas present, but I had spoiled his surprise. This is still a talked about matter to this day! I made a delicious pork roast with mashed potatoes and gravy. One of the guys, David Kumnick, said to Ray, "Something is wrong with this gravy; it doesn't have lumps in it!" Evidently, when Ray cooked for the three of them, he had lumps in the gravy!

Our school year began with Ray teaching Industrial Arts, and I taught some English classes, Social Studies, and music. It was a gratifying year with a lot of close associations with our students and faculty. They were often in our home for Bible study and social gatherings. In the middle of the year, the house next door became empty. It was a more permanent home built with wood frame construction and Masonite siding, so we moved in. It was nice to get out of the bush house as they were harder to clean, and it seemed like more fleas and bugs got in. Our water was from a tank (holding 1000 gallons) connected to our roof from which the water would fall. We had to be careful if we didn't have rain for a while, we might run out of water, and it would have to be carried up from the river.

Eunice and Ray's first home they lived in after they were married. 1966

Wash day for Eunice

Eunice cutting Ray's hair, December 1969

*The infamous spice rack (5 decades later!), that created
the first disruption to marital bliss!*

CHAPTER 21

Back to the U.S.

We made arrangements with the mission to fly to the U.S. and Australia during our December – January school break that year. We paid our own way since we weren't due for furlough. We really wanted to meet each other's family. I wanted Ray to see some of the cities I had seen around the world. We decided to fly via Thailand, New Delhi, Athens, Rome, Cologne, Paris, London, New York. We enjoyed all of our stops. We saw the Golden Ships, Thailand's king, and tasted all the delicious spiced food. We met friendly people who made it a special place. New Delhi was beautiful as we toured the Taj Mahal, ate spiced dishes with hot condiments, but we were saddened by the many people lying in the streets begging. Then on to Greece. Athens was a beautiful city on the sea. We rented a cab to take us around the city. We only had a seven-hour layover. We saw the Acropolis and the beautiful sights of the city. From the shore, the water was so beautiful and blue. Then on to Rome, where we toured the city and St. Peter's Cathedral, Trevi Fountain, the Colosseum, Appian Way, and the Catacombs. All were very beautiful.

From there, we traveled to Frankfort, Germany, where we toured the city's highlights: the market, a German restaurant with a lot of singing German songs with gusto, and the Cologne

Church, which was still being rebuilt after being bombed in World War II. Then on to Paris, France, where we toured Mater Dei Cathedral, The Louvre, the Eifel Tower, and down the Champs de Elysée to the Arc de Triomphe. To London, where we saw the changing of the guard at Buckingham Palace, rode the double-decker busses through the city, and visited Nelson's Square. Then, to the Tower of London to see the Crown jewels. We went on to Westminster Abbey, where kings and queens are buried, and there was beautiful architecture to admire.

Finally, we made the flight across the ocean to New York and Ray's first sighting of the US. We viewed the Statue of Liberty as we were landing. To meet us at the airport were forty people from Hope Lutheran Church, Levittown, Pennsylvania, the people who supported me so well in Papua New Guinea. They were as excited to meet Ray as he was to meet them. They took us to a lovely restaurant, and the conversation was nonstop about work for Jesus and their involvement in supplying us to be able to do it. We spent three days with them, and it was a faith-strengthening time. Our praises to God rang out loud and clear. Ray was amazed at their love for us.

Then we flew on to St Louis and spent a wonderful four weeks. Ray got to know my family and the many church members from Bethlehem-Ferrin, Trinity-Hoffman, Messiah-Carlyle, Trinity-Hoyleton, St. John-New Minden, Trinity-Nashville, and Trinity-Centralia who had supported us.

We showed slides and spoke in all these places and others. We expressed our gratefulness for all their support in letters and money over the previous years.

We had many family get-togethers and fun times, even went bowling together. Then came the time to leave, and there were tears, especially to say goodbye to mother as she was in failing health and we might not see her again on this earth, but we knew she was safely in the arms of Jesus, many prayers were said.

We flew to San Francisco. Ray met the Raffs, Betty, David, and family, and we had two beautiful days with them. The love of our Lord Jesus was evident, so we prayed and shared with them. They took us, especially Ray, on a sightseeing adventure, and we saw the Golden Gate Bridge, Alcatraz, rode on the cable car on the hill downtown, and ate at Fisherman's Wharf. We also visited their church, which had many Chinese members. Betty was involved in doing a lot of helpful services there. She taught ladies Bible class, Sunday School, and visited people in jail.

Then we flew on to Oahu, Hawaii, and had two wonderful days there. We toured the island, saw sugar cane and pineapple fields; we visited the downed ships of World War II, and had a fun time on the beach.

Then it was on to a stop at Fiji for refueling and on to Sydney and Brisbane. Ray's sister, Thora, and her friend, June, and Ray's friend, George Ost, met us. It was our first meeting, but they treated me like family. We then drove over a very bumpy bridge, several miles to Redcliffe, at 7 Henry Street, where Ray's parents lived.

There was a lot of love and hugs. We spent a week with them. I met all of Ray's family: his brothers: Alva, wife Noela, and sons Greg, Jeffrey, and Andrew; his sister Joyce and her husband, Nelson. I had met sister Selma and family at our wedding and on our honeymoon. We had a wonderful time there; Ray's parents lived five blocks from the beach.

Then we drove up to Toowoomba, where Ray lived until he was seven, on a farm with twenty feet of topsoil. Toowoomba is a beautiful flower city, one-hundred miles from Redcliffe. Every

September, the jacaranda flowers were in full bloom when they have the "Carnival of Flowers." Ray's dad and mom retired to Redcliffe from Toowoomba. It was summer, and the flowers in Toowoomba were in full bloom. We passed a lot of fruit stands along the road up, and the fruit that impressed me most was the plump, delicious apricots. Queensland is a tropical state, so delicious pineapple, grapefruit, oranges, and berries, were everywhere, as well as fresh vegetables.

Ray and I did several New Guinea presentations in the area. At one of them, I got very dizzy, and Ray had to finish the lecture. Two days later, we learned that I was pregnant. This was a great joy, and we could share it with Ray's family. Then it was sad to say goodbye, but we needed to get back to New Guinea to get ready for school. We got our flight to Port Moresby but had to wait a day to get a flight to Mt. Hagen and Wapenamanda. We stayed in Port Moresby overnight with Roland Weier, who gave us his single bed. Well, it was a little narrow, but we were so tired we slept reasonably well.

Our flight the next day to Mt. Hagen and Wapenamanda, again was a DC-3 with cargo in the middle and our row seats against the wall of the plane. Ed Dicke and his crew met us at Wapenamanda and took us in a jeep over to Pausa. We were happy to be in our home again. The staff at St. Paul's Lutheran High School gave us a warm welcome. We were very busy the next week as we got ready for school and our students' arrival.

By this time, we had over one hundred boys and thirty girls in our school. It was a joy teaching the students. Ray was back at his Industrial Arts classroom, and I taught English and Social Studies classes. In June, Ray and Don Yarroll, fellow teacher, went to the Sepik area to learn about their art and life. They built very ornate spirit houses to worship their spirits. They came back just plastered with mosquito bites. The doctor gave them extra chloroquine and medicated salve to ease the pain and itching. They recovered quickly.

CHAPTER 22

Paula Arrives

We were looking forward to August and the arrival of our baby. On Saturday, August 17th, I went into labor. By Sunday morning, I was still in labor but with no results. Many of the single staff came to visit Sunday afternoon. Sunday evening, things moved a little faster but too slow for Dr. MacArthur and his wife. They were walking the floor, but I didn't know why. It turned out that he was worried because he was not a surgeon and couldn't do a cesarean surgery. They were calling an aircraft to fly me to the hospital in Goroka in the morning as soon as it would get to be daylight. God took care of me, and at 4 AM, my labor got harder. By 4:30 AM, we had a little girl, Paula Ann. We stayed at the hospital six days, as in those days, they kept mothers that long to make sure of no complications.

Now our life changed as we had a little one to take care of. We were well supplied with all of the baby necessities. They came in Charlie Chip cans from our dear ones at Levittown, Pennsylvania: Len and Ruth Pitney, Neil and Alice Werberig, and Howard and Carolyn Deufendach along with others who collected, packed, and sent all we needed. We lacked nothing. Paula was a healthy little girl! We were so thankful to God for her. She was the third baby at our station born in August. Dottie Schaus had delivered a little girl a few days before, and Ruth Budke had delivered a little boy, so we did a lot of comparing how to care for babies.

CHAPTER 23

Ray's Parents Visit

At Christmas in 1968, Ray's parents, sister Thora, and sister Selma with her daughter Sandy and cousin Rosalind Vahrenkamp visited us. They had such a good time getting acquainted with everyone in New Guinea. We had many evening get-togethers at our house with student visitors and mission staff. The students did a Muum for them – cooking in a hole in the ground on banana leaves. We supplied a ham: the New Guineans gave us a chicken, and we bought potatoes and sweet potatoes from New Guineans who brought them to our house.

We drove them up the valley to see some of our mission stations, our hospital in Mambisanda, and the business office at Wapenamanda. Then we went to the agriculture station at Mukutamanda and our school for missionary children at Amapyaka, where their grandson, John Weier, Selma, and Russell's son, was sent from Menyamya to school. It was tough for a young boy to be so far from home. On weekends he stayed with his uncle Don and Gaye Weier. After an incredible two weeks, we flew with them out to Madang on the coast, our mission vacation spot. As we were leaving, a jeep door was slammed on Ray's mother's hand. She had a lot of pain but no broken fingers or bones. On our flight to Madang, the pilot noticed that Paula was suffering and he knew that it was probably her ears bothering her, so he said he would fly as low as he could to prevent ear damage. By God's mercy, this was another very special treatment we received.

Madang was a respite. We went to the beach, ate at a wonderful New Guinean restaurant where we were entertained with New Guinean dancers and music. Of course, the frangipani trees were in bloom, plus many other beautiful trees and plants. After five beautiful days, we bid them goodbye as they flew back to Brisbane, and we flew back up to the Western Highlands.

CHAPTER 24

Charla Arrives

After we got back, we learned that I was pregnant again, so I was pretty much a full-time mother. Ray was back to teaching Industrial Arts, and I was busy keeping our home going and often served New Guineans who had wounds and other light ailments.

On August 30th, our second little girl, Charla Lynn, arrived. The labor was very fast with her. We named her after our friend Garry Wolf's wife, Charla. Garry had gone home and returned married about a month before our Charla was born, and Ray liked the name. Now my life got busier, but we were very happy.

After Charla could walk, I started a preschool with our small children on the station. This was a success, and I did it for three years until we left New Guinea.

One day Paula and Charla and Paul and Glenn Schmeling wandered off and got to the hill above Ray's classroom. It had a six-foot drop at the bottom. They decided to roll down the hill. Luckily, Ray saw them and ran out to stop them halfway down the hill, or we may have had a tragedy. Thank you, Lord!

Sometimes Ray and I and the girls would get on a motorbike and ride to visit other mission families up the valley, especially the Janetski's, who were like parents to us. Now we think how dangerous that was!

CHAPTER 25

Life at Pausa

Things went well at St. Paul's Lutheran High School. Ray taught the students to make items like tables, chairs, cupboards, and shelves they could use in the classroom. The New Guineans were also starting to live in houses with wooden floors and could use these items.

On Sunday, the students would march up the hill from their dormitories carrying a large cross singing "Onward Christian Soldiers" They would pick up the faculty and families on the way; it was very uplifting to walk down to the classroom/church all singing together. We had a pastor and several teachers who could deliver good sermons so our worship would lift our spirits.

Staff member Connie Pucci had a little house near the girl's dormitory. Another staff member lived near the boy's dormitories. There were times when a student would have an anxiety attack at night, and it woke us all up, and we gathered to comfort and pray with him, sing with him, and most of the time, they would settle down and go back to sleep. We never left until we were sure they were asleep. We loved the students like our own children.

During this time, a serious faction arose in our mission. Some of our new missionaries arriving from the U.S. were teaching that creation was not seven days but a period of time that allowed for evolution. They taught the Jonah story as a fable and the virgin birth of Jesus as not really happening as well as other false teachings.

Well, I knew from the Bible; this was not true. So, I spoke up and wrote a paper telling them they were not preaching and teaching the True Word of God. I was ostracized and given some harsh words of admonition, but I did not waver.

When we returned to the U.S., we learned that these teachings were creeping into our seminary in St. Louis. We knew this was a serious problem. We joined laymen who were fighting these teachings at our Concordia Seminary, St. Louis. It ended up that those professors teaching these doctrines walked out of the seminary. It saved our seminary, and they got back to teaching the Bible as the true, inspired, word of God; we must never detract from the Bible or add to it. Revelation 22:18-19 NIV *"I warn everyone who hears the words of the prophecy of this book: If anyone adds anything to them, God will add to him the plagues described in this book. And if anyone takes words away from this book of prophecy, God will take away from him his share in the tree of life and in the holy city, which are described in this book."*

The students marched from their dormitory carrying a cross and picking up Eunice and Ray, and faculty members and marched to their church/classroom building singing "Onward Christian Soldiers". A regular Sunday morning service occurrence.

St. Paul's Lutheran High School baptism Pausa at the Lai River.

Baptism at the Lai River St. Paul's Lutheran High School

Chapter 26

A Visit to Australia

In December 1970, we decided to go to Australia during school break as Ray's parents were celebrating their 50th wedding anniversary. The celebration was held at Ray's sister, Joyce's, home in Toowoomba. A delicious meal and fruit cake were served. We were able to meet many more of Ray's relatives, family and friends.

What a great six weeks it was as we had family time with Ray's family. We went to Tarango Park and saw the parakeets. They gave us pans of bread and honey to hold, and the birds flew on our arms to eat it. They also had koala bears, kangaroos, wallabies, wombats, and other animals to see. There were also pigeons on the ground, and Charla, just learning to walk, loved to chase them. We rode the train in the park and had a happy time.

When we left, we had to walk from the airport to the plane. A photographer was there from their newspaper and television station, so Ray's parents saw us that evening on TV. They said we were missionary warriors going back to the island of New Guinea, which Australians knew was very primitive, so we got a good review!

Paula and Charla riding kangaroos at Torango Park, near Brisbane. Australia.

Charla and a Koala Bear

CHAPTER 27

Life in New Guinea

Life in New Guinea moved on as usual. Ray had a big garden and grew most of our vegetables and bananas, strawberries, pawpaw, pineapples, etc. I had a gardenia plant in the middle of his garden, which he was not fond of as it disturbed his plant arrangement!

We had delicious meals. Our meat came up once a month on a freezer run by air from a meat-market at Lutmis (import, export) store in Madang. We could get lamb roast, hamburger, ham, and pork roast. It was expensive, so we ordered very little and made it last.

We were fortunate to have a refrigerator at our station at Pausa and Mambisanda where the hospital was. There was a hydroelectric plant built below a waterfall between the two stations that supplied the electricity. Before the plant was built, our refrigerator ran on kerosene.

We drank a lot of lemonade and Passion fruit drink. We ordered cookies (biscuits) in tin boxes, 12" x 12" x 10" from Lutmis also, imported from Australia. They were Arnotts and tasted terrific and stayed fresh. I often thought back to my first years in New Guinea when I taught my cook boy to make bread and had peanut butter and jelly sandwiches, tinned cheese that came in a can, sandwiches, and canned foods but very little as they were very expensive!

CHAPTER 28

The Final New Guinea Graduation

We would have graduation at the end of each year, and it would be a big ceremony. The boys wore white shirts and black shorts, the girls wore a piece of cloth around their waist which hung down to their knees and a blouse over the top. After not wearing many clothes, they were getting very acquainted with wearing clothing and loved it. They did not wear shoes, but those came later, mostly flip flops. We always had a speaker, choir students who had learned tunes and were now singing very well and in harmony, and the principal handing out diplomas. We formed a congratulation reception line and then had a luncheon. We staff wives would make many sandwiches, biscuits, and lemonade. Wonderful times!!

St. Paul's Lutheran High School Graduation November 1968. Notice the two girls graduating for first time.

CHAPTER 29

Furlough – Return to the U.S.

Then in 1971, we had to start thinking about furlough. Would we come back to New Guinea? It took deep prayer and contemplation. It became apparent that Ray was being replaced by New Guineans, who were now Industrial Art teachers during the year. They still needed me to teach English, but we were led through prayer to return to either the U.S. or Australia. Ray liked teaching a lot but had no degree; he had a four-year apprenticeship in building arts. So, we applied to colleges in Australia and the U.S. We got the best response from Southern Illinois University in Carbondale, Illinois. They would give Ray two years of credit for his apprenticeship. So, thank God that decision was made!

It was hard for the last months! We knew we loved our New Guinea people and students. They were now our people. Paula and Charla were happy there, but Paula would have to go to boarding school when she was six, and we dreaded that.

There were a lot of parties and farewell occasions in November. We were sad to leave our mission family and the New Guinea people and students. We needed winter coats for Paula and Charla since it would be winter on our way to America. I could only get spring coats at David Jones in Australia as it was summer, but it was better than nothing!

So, in December, we packed what we could in barrels and sent it to Ray's parents in Australia as the mission would not send it to the U.S. since Ray was Australian. So, we flew into Brisbane to stay with Ray's parents while we got a green card for Ray. This card was necessary for non-citizens who wanted to live in the U.S. We had registered Paula and Charla at birth with both U.S. and Australian citizenship. God was leading and guiding us. We trusted Him. Ray and I had to go to Sydney to get his green card at the American Embassy. We got it in two days. We left the girls with Ray's parents in Brisbane, and when we got back, it was a matter of getting our tickets for America. We decided to go home via Hong Kong and Japan, then into Minnesota. From there, we would fly to St. Louis.

It was hard to say goodbye to Ray's family once again. There were lots of hugs and tears. We arrived in Hong Kong and stayed in a beautiful hotel; the Chinese know how to make a place attractive! So many hangings with symbols of gold on red silk. There were spirals with shiny silver, red and black designs. We toured Hong Kong for two days. Since I had been there before, I knew my way a little, and we even took the bus into Kowloon. The streets were decorated so beautifully, and we took Paula and Charla in the stores to pick one thing to take home. As usual, the Chinese people were very kind and loved Paula and Charla with their blond hair.

Then it was on to Japan. My friend, Phyllis Chamberlain, was a missionary there and wanted us to stay with her. She took us all around Tokyo. We saw Mount Fuji, the highest mountain in Japan, very clearly – unusual as it is often cloud covered. We ate at a Japanese restaurant, sat on the floor at a table where food was cooked for us at the end of the table, it was very delicious! Paula and Charla were again an attraction with their very blonde hair as we strolled the streets. Everyone wanted to touch their hair. The people were very friendly. Many were lighting candles and burning incense at the Buddha temples along the way. Phyllis said, "We are working hard to tell them about Jesus." The walk-ways were all very crowded with people. After three days, we bid farewell and flew on to Minnesota to the home of Ruth and Len Pitney, who were like parents to me in Levittown. They had now retired in Park Rapids, Minnesota, their home before Levittown and where they both grew up.

We landed in Minneapolis. It was cold, there was snow on the ground, but they had warm coats for all of us, which our Levit-town friends had sent. We spent three terrific days with them. Paula, Charla, and Ray got acquainted with snow. They even built a snowman. Some relatives of the Pitney's gave us warm sweaters, slacks, and socks. The Pitney's got boots for all of us and gloves. We were so thankful for all their goodness. Ruth is a good cook and made great meals, especially a beef roast with all the right vegetables! They also took us to a lumber camp where we had a meal with the lumbermen using tin utensils and plates. But the slapjacks and bacon were delicious! We prayed and thanked God for His marvelous blessings to all of us.

Back to the airport, a long drive from Park Rapids to Minne-apolis. Charla got her head between two balusters on the staircase as we went down the steps to the planes, and Ray worked hard to get her head out. We almost missed the plane for St. Louis, but we were thankful Charla was okay. We landed in St. Louis, quite happy that there were no more flights. Luther and Eileen, my brother and sister-in-law, met us. It was late afternoon, and we were tired, but it was still a sixty-mile ride to their home in Shattuc, Illinois.

We stopped at sister Erna and her husband Paul Tyberendt's home. All my siblings were there, except Betty. Erna cooked a delicious roast beef dinner with chocolate pie for dessert. Paula and Charla really liked the pie. We stayed at Luther and Eileen's house for a few days. Wilma (my sister) and Willard Maschhoff had a vacant farmhouse we could live in, so we were delighted. It took a few days to fix it up, but Ray is a good carpenter, so it went quickly. We went to buy a car in Centralia and found a used Ford Pinto in good shape.

I recall a joyous occasion in winter, during December. My brother, Luther, who worked for TW airlines, asked, "Would you like some goldfish?" "Of Course!" I said. He explained that some fish had come in on a flight, and they were frozen, but if I wanted some, he would bring them over. When he brought them to our little house, he had eight large containers of frozen goldfish. Well, I never expected this, so I called my sister and sister-in-law to bring some washtubs. We filled seven tubs with frozen fish. We put the fish in our entry and living room as we had little space in the small farmhouse. As they thawed, the fish became alive, and soon, we had seven tubs of lively goldfish. We started asking our relatives and friends – "Would you like goldfish?" We gave many of them away and had fun doing it. Lee's Variety store, a local establishment in Nashville, Illinois, wondered why they had a run on their fish tanks. It was quite an experience and a favorite memory today because we had so much fun giving away the fish.

CHAPTER 30

Carbondale, Illinois

Then Ray and I went to Southern Illinois University in Carbondale to register and enroll him for school. We had arrived home on January 2nd, and he would start school on January 15th, 1972. From Hoyleton, where the farmhouse was, to Carbondale was about sixty miles, so we rented an apartment for a few months. While in Carbondale, the girls missed New Guinea. One day Paula said, very firmly: "I want to go back to New Guinea and never come back here!"

One day the girls were playing with two boys from South Korea. They ran along the apartments where some windows were open. Charla bumped into a window and got a severe gash in her forehead. It bled heavily, and we rushed her to the hospital. She was admitted, but they wouldn't let Ray and I go with her into the treatment room. It broke my heart as she cried so hard. They put in stitches, and she recovered with only a minor scar.

CHAPTER 31
Nursing Home Employment

By the end of March, I needed to go to work. So, we moved into our farmhouse, and Ray rented a mobile home at SIU. Ray settled into school very well, even with the Australian accent! I got a job at Friendship Manor Nursing Home in Nashville. Sister Wilma took care of Paula and Charla while I was working. I was happy to be at the nursing home since my mother was a resident there and I could see her every day. The work was hard, but I was thankful for a job.

Eunice's siblings: Wilma, Wilbert, Eunice, Richard, Luther, Erna, Betty

CHAPTER 32

Trinity, Hoffman

In August, I got a job teaching at Trinity Lutheran School in Hoffman, grades one and two. I was happy to be teaching again. Since my Uncle Fred Redeker had taught at Hoffman many years before, I felt at home being there. My Aunt Augusta also had taught there. At this time, Paula was ready to go to kindergarten, so we sent her to Trinity Lutheran School in Hoyleton; it was closer to our home and Wilma's home. Wilma helped us a lot with things for the girls.

Ray would come home Friday afternoon till Monday morning; those were precious times. Ray is a good gardener, so he put in a garden for us. It helped us so much to have fresh vegetables, strawberries, and rhubarb from our garden. I canned a lot of green beans, tomatoes, and pickles.

That winter, in February, we had a huge snowfall, with very large drifts. We were blocked in, but our good neighbor, Orville Heseman, came with his big tractor and dug us out. For smaller snows, my brother-in-law, Willard, would come to clear our driveway. We bought a new gas stove from a friend to heat our first floor, it worked pretty well.

Ray finished his studies with a Bachelor's degree after one year and two semesters, so he was ready for a job. SIU helped him get an Industrial Arts job at Delavan High School in Delavan, Illinois.

Since I did not want to leave Hoffman school without due notice, Ray moved up to Delavan in September, and the girls and I moved up at the end of December. Paula transferred to Delavan public school, and Charla, now in kindergarten, also to Delavan public. I was not happy as I wanted our girls to go to a Lutheran school to learn about Jesus and study God's Word and other subjects. I got some teaching fill-in jobs at San Jose, Illinois, the next year.

In February of that year, Ray and I went to a seminar at Zion Lutheran Church in Lincoln, Illinois, where Reverend A. Goldberger was the pastor. Reverend Pflug was the speaker. He was from our Concordia seminary for pastors at Springfield, Illinois. We were very impressed with the fellowship building at Lincoln. The upstairs was like a gym and had a large stage on one end. The basement had eight Sunday School rooms. I said to Ray, "We can start a Lutheran School here." We talked to Rev. Goldberger and Rev. Pflug after the service about a school in this wonderful building. Pastor Goldberger seemed to be a little taken aback, but Pastor Pflug said, "Yes, why don't you have a school? You have a great building." So, Pastor Goldberger invited me to a school board meeting the next Monday evening.

I got a mixed reception, but not all negative. It so happened that a member of the board had a grandson that was dying of Rhys disease. Before we closed, I led the group in a prayer and had each one of them say a prayer. The next morning, I had a call from Helen Haseley, a board of education member, that the little boy, Chad Goldhammer, had taken a turn in the night and was doing very well. God was just helping me to open the door to starting a school.

They called another meeting in May. It was controversial, but they said if I could get twelve students, they would open the school. Well, I made many calls in the next two months, and at our meeting on July 20th, I had only nine commitments for first and second grade and five for kindergarten. By the grace of God, they said, "We will start the school."

I had been principal at Levittown and started a school in New Guinea. Now, I was given the job of principal at Lincoln. I had three summers in administration courses at Temple University in Philadelphia while in Levittown, so I had an excellent background to do this. Starting a school in one month was a challenge, but don't worry; God is in charge!

We hired Mildred Maaks for kindergarten. Dona Sauer was teaching preschool, which had been in existence there for several years. I ordered books and other supplies and felt so blessed when we heard the Lutheran School at Schaumberg, Illinois, was closing and had all their desks and school furniture for sale. Well, two school board members went with me. Gene Aukamp had a big farm truck, and we loaded up twenty-one desks, a teacher's desk, and several bookcases. God kept strengthening my faith – how could all this happen?

Then we decided to knock out a wall and make two Sunday School rooms into a larger classroom. It had a gray brick wall, so we decided to paint it light blue. We were still painting two days before school started on August 22nd. The pastor's house, a large three-story house next door to the school, was empty, and the congregation agreed to let us live there. Our good friends from Delavan; the Hauptlis, the Groenewalds, Uncle Andy Kunkle, and Mary Jurgen, moved us from our apartment in Delavan to Lincoln. They were such a happy, lively group that we had fun moving. A couple of older ladies helped clean the parsonage, so we had a lovely big home.

Being next door to school helped a lot, as Paula and Charla could go home or stay at school with me. The lady next door, Mrs. Girard, who was friendly to the pastors, became an excellent friend. She had a beautiful cat, Krissy, that Paula and Charla loved. We also had a cat named Goldie. Mrs. Girard often brought Ray a box of donuts when he shoveled her snow.

Ruth and Len Pitney with Paula on her first day of school at Trinity Lutheran School, Hoyleton, Illinois. Ruth and Len were Eunice's second parents.

CHAPTER 33

Another School Beginning

School got off to a good start, with nine in my class, five in kindergarten, and ten in preschool. We played in the parking lot and, when rainy, upstairs in the lovely gym. I did a lot to keep the children in front of the congregation by singing every Sunday. They sang "Children of the Heavenly Father" many times. We presented a Christmas play and an Easter play. For nine children, they sang beautifully. The plays I wrote were filled with Bible verses. God gave me nine brilliant children. When God wants anything to go forward, He provides everything you need. I was in constant prayer.

As the year ended, all had gone very well, so we opened enrollment for the next year, and thirty enrolled for grades three and four, twenty-one for first and second grade, and fifteen for kindergarten.

My soul just praised God! His presence was so visible to us. We knocked a wall out between two more classrooms and bought furnishings for that room. We called another teacher, Curtis Boehne, a new graduate. So, my workload was getting very heavy being principal and teaching, but I had an outstanding secretary, Mrs. Mary Ellen Schreiber. Good secretaries make a principal look good!

That year went very well. We had the children regularly sing in church and also perform Christmas and Easter programs. We also did a few special services during the year. At the end of that year, we again opened enrollment and had twenty-four enroll for grades five and six. This was another miracle!

We had to knock another wall out and get another classroom ready. We called another teacher Mr. Kim Eggerman. Since the workload was getting pretty heavy for me, we called Mr. Eggerman as principal. That gave me more time with family and to be a witness to people. We again did a lot of programs in front of the congregation during the year. Since we were filled, with no more rooms to expand, we started talking about building a school. The congregation had leased property on Woodland road, the main road into town. It was an ideal school location. We hired an architect, Malanski Litvan, from Springfield, Illinois, who designed plans for us. After several meetings, we had a good plan, and we hired a builder.

Before we got started, the landowner decided he wanted the property back because it was prime land for development. Lincoln was expanding to the west as the Interstate had just been put in around the city. (The school was to be located in this direction). We called a congregational meeting, and I was worried we wouldn't get the school building. So more praying and telling the Lord, "Your will be done." There was a lot of discussion at the meeting, pro and con. By God's grace, the conclusion came to: we had one year left on the lease, and so if we started building the school, it would be completed within the year, and the land would be ours. We could also now open enrollment for the next year. As a result of the new registrations, we had around twenty-five to thirty for seventh and eighth grade.

Well, I knew God was in control here. We built the building and dedicated it on April 1st, 1980. Rev Walter Maier, Jr., who had been my pastor in Levittown, was the speaker. We had a large crowd for the ceremony; the gym was overflowing. There were lots of hugs after the service, so many supporters. Even our friends from Delavan and other places had come.

During this year, Mr. Eggerman took a call, and we called Mr. David Guenhagen as principal and teacher of grades seven and eight. We also called a teacher for fifth and sixth grade, Mr. David Kleimola.

CHAPTER 34

Zion Lutheran School, Lincoln, Illinois Opens

Our new building was a state-of-the-art building. I had helped with the Levittown school building and had a concept of what a school should have. We and the planners who designed the school had five objectives in mind: 1) To provide a pleasant learning environment. 2) To provide a degree of separation of lower grades and higher grades. 3) To provide for the maximum utilization of every square foot of the building. 4) To provide multi-use space for the church and community to bring the entire Christian fellowship into contact with the school. 5) To provide a building form that would easily accommodate future expansion.

The building was divided into two major areas, the academic/administration areas, and the multi-purpose and support facilities. The heart of the academic area, the core, contained a multimedia learning center and an audiovisual science room. Clustered on either side of the core were preschool and the lower grade classroom cluster, and the upper-grade classrooms. The school offices and teachers' workroom were within a few steps of these learning areas. Immediately across the central hallway were the all-purpose and support areas. The all-purpose room with adjacent dressing rooms provided an indoor physical education area which would accommodate scholastic and sporting events. The all-purpose room was convertible into an auditorium using the dual-purpose stage/music practice area and moveable seating.

The lunchroom with adjacent kitchen facilities also opened into the all-purpose room for school lunches or Christian fellowship dining. The academic area's separation from the all-purpose/support functions allowed easy access for community use without disturbing the prime educational process.

It was with great joy that we moved into our new school. It was like a dream to have plenty of space and places for all activities. A lot of creative ideas arose to utilize the building. We had art shows, science display evening, and the students put on little plays for parents and one big play at the end of the year. The Parent Teacher League also had a fund-raising pancake meal each year. This created additional funding for the school. All this was good to keep the people seeing the school and being part of it and getting them to see what God can do. Ray and I were thanking God daily that Paula and Charla were going to a Christian school and had terrific Christian friends to encourage them in their faith.

Zion Lutheran School Lincoln, Illinois

Eunice's first class at Zion Lutheran School, Lincoln, Illinois. September 1974

Tapestry made by Mrs. Elaine Ray for Zion Lutheran School Dedication.

Words from the Pastor on Dedication
Day of Zion Lutheran School, Lincoln, IL

With grateful hearts we thank God for His mercy and guidance as we dedicate this new school to His glory. We thank Him for moving the members of this congregations to build this school so that children can be brought to the Lord Jesus and have a deep and abiding faith.

We are truly indebted to many, and our Heavnly Father knows who all prayed and worked for this project. I am compelled to acknowledge the encouragement and inspiration given by Mrs. Eunice Hauster. I also feel compelled to mention the tremendous amount of work and time given by both Ivan Ray who literally gave himself to the erection of this building and to Eugene Aukamp who saw that the furnishing and necessities were acquired.

Volunteers painted the 3/4 mile of walls 3 coats and installed all ceiling tiles. Others painted the doors and the door frames while others scrubbed and cleaned. Some did electrical work at the lift station, on the intercom system and the public address system. Many people literally helped to build this school.

We must note that in addition to the financial contributions, the congregation has raised investments for the Central Illinois District Church Extension Fund in the amount of $600,000. (Another $150,000 is needed for a reduced rate of interest on our loan.) In doing this, a record was set by raising over a half million in investments within one year. This is a record in the district and perhaps in the synod.

A long list of people who in some way helped could be made, but instead I just want to say "Thank You" for such splendid cooperation and help. May God bless you, for I know that everything you did, you did out of love to the Lord Jesus Christ who first loved us and gave Himself to the death of the cross for us.

Eunice teaching First and Second grade in new Lutheran School, Lincoln, Illinois.

Zion Lutheran School, Lincoln, Illinois, 40th Anniversary

CHAPTER 35
God Sends More Family

In 1979, our Zion congregation became aware of many Vietnamese people on the waters in boats around the country of Vietnam: and they would all die unless adopted. These people paid a high price to get on these boats. The government was cruel to them. So, our church proceeded with the adoption process. We had several ladies in our church, especially Dorothy Lehner, Elaine Ray, Margaret Minder, and Norma Hein, who did much of the paperwork with Lutheran Immigration. After several months they assigned a family to us. Since we had moved out of the parsonage to a house on Eleventh Street, the parsonage was available for a Vietnamese family. It was a cold November night when they arrived by air in Springfield, Illinois. Ray and I had gotten involved, so we were also there to greet them. We got a mother, Kim, with nine children; some were nieces and nephews. They were Susan, David, Michael and Steven and two other boys who did not stay with us; they had relatives in Massachusetts. The last three arrived three months later.

We got them all settled in the parsonage. Our Vietnamese family was so lost. Everything was so strange to them. But the congregation took good care of them, and little by little, they adjusted. The mother, Kim, wanted to work right away, so she got a job cleaning at the hospital. Three of the children were enrolled in Zion Lutheran School and two in Lincoln High School. Steven was six years old and in my first and second-grade classroom. Fortunately, we had a Chinese teacher at Lincoln College who knew Mandarin and helped us until they began to learn English.

After several months the father, Quam, came with their daughter, Mary, who was twenty years old. Mary knew English, so Lennard Lehner, a church member, got her a secretarial job at the prison where he worked. Due to family difficulties, Quam moved to Massachusetts where he had other relatives.

They were a remarkable group and adjusted quickly to American life. As soon as the high school students graduated, they got jobs. All were hard workers. They all took catechism with Pastor Goldberger and joined Zion Lutheran Church. Ray and I got close to the family as we had known Chinese merchants at the coast in Papua New Guinea; we knew God was giving us these people to lead them to Him. They were in Lincoln for about ten years, and then they moved to Houston, Texas, where they knew some people and enjoy a warmer climate and joined the LCMS church there.

Mary married Peter Ngo, a refugee adopted by a church in Grand Rapids, Michigan. They had a beautiful wedding in Houston, Texas. Ray and I were able to attend. Mary became a travel agent and eventually became a mother to their son, Peter Junior.

Susan got a degree in physical therapy and still works at a Hospital in Houston today. She married Darrell Valentine; they have a daughter, Sarah. David got a job at a Houston airport and advanced to being in charge of maintenance.

Michael worked at Burger King and became a manager, but then got a job as a graphic designer and still does that work. He married Hoa La Ond from Vietnam, and they have five children:

Jessica, Lissa, Christina, Sophia, and Jayden. They have all visited us many times.

Steven got an engineering degree at Rose Hulman University in Terre Haute, Indiana. I visited him often to make sure he was doing okay. He lives in Houston and Brazil. Peter Jr. also went to Rose Hulman and got a degree in engineering; I often visited him also. He works for the military in Bloomfield, Indiana.

They have been a success all the way, and we thank and praise God that He sent them to us.

CHAPTER 36

Ray's Citizenship

After two years in our new school, Ray was in difficulty because of citizenship. The rule was that after five years, you had to get your citizenship to teach at Delavan High School. It was now seven years, and Ray did not have his citizenship, so he applied, but it took about two years to get it, so he was let go from the high school.

We decided to move back to Hoyleton while Ray was waiting for citizenship. I could get a job again at Trinity Lutheran School in Hoffman, Illinois. Ray was offered a construction job at Hoffman Lumber by Bob Michael, the owner. We loved our house on Eleventh Street in Lincoln, but knew we had to move.

Paula and Charla were enrolled at Trinity Lutheran, Hoyleton but missed their friends and school in Lincoln. I enjoyed my work at Trinity Hoffman. Ray enjoyed his work building sheds, but one day a 2x4 that he was standing on 16 feet above the ground, broke, and he fell onto a concrete floor. He broke his ankle and was very bruised. Ray went on worker's compensation. He had started his citizenship application at Lincoln, actually Chicago, through the American Embassy, but somehow everything was lost when we moved to Hoyleton, so we started again.

Now we were working through the Federal Building in East St. Louis. I knew a senator from Southern Illinois, from Walther League, so we asked him for help, and then things moved quickly. Ray had gotten his Master's Degree while teaching at Lincoln. He got notice of being sworn in as a citizen on November 27th, 1984. I took off from school, and so did Paula and Charla. This was a very big day and occasion. A praise God day! Ray was now ready to teach again. But after his leg healed, initially he took a job with Herschel Kasten making stakes. Ray did this for about three years, then Herschel knew a political Committeeman very well, and the Committeeman helped Ray get a teaching job at Centralia Correctional Center. He was hired as a Graphic Arts teacher and worked there until he retired in 2000.

Ray building their house at New Minden, Illinois. 1982

Ray's birthday cake, the Australian flag.

Ray and Paula

Ray is now an American citizen.

CHAPTER 37

Our Silver Wedding Anniversary

On November 26th, 1991, we celebrated our 25th wedding anniversary. We had the celebration in the gym at Trinity Lutheran School, Hoffman, Illinois. It was such a happy occasion! Rev. Jim Herzog gave the sermon, and Rev. Timothy Mueller, of St. John's New Minden, was the liturgist. The Wayne Maschhoff's and Robert Poirot's cooked pork chops for everyone. This was a big feat since it was a cold day. A group of ladies cooked the rest of the dinner.

A special guest was our student Kapaa and his wife from Papua New Guinea and now an ambassador to the United Nations in New York. My maid of honor, Loretta Adler, and her husband, Dick, who served as best man, came from St. Louis. Bridesmaid Janice Haby Schubert came from Adelaide, Australia. Garry Wolff, our groomsman, and wife Charla came from Altamont, Illinois. Ray's sister, Thora, came from Toowoomba, Australia, and our missionary friends Althea Weier Milbrath from Milwaukee, and Rev. Clarence and Ruth Budke from Asheville, North Carolina, also came.

Flowers and gifts came from Levittown, Pennsylvania. My family: brothers, sisters, aunts, uncles, nieces, and nephews were all there. Dennis and Carol Knauer, Doris and Emma Knauer,

Bob Huelskoetter, Martin and Kathy Roos, Gene and Shirley Aukamp, Carl and Norma Heins, Vernon and Helen Haseby, Irene Franz, Earl and Margaret Mendor all came from Lincoln, Illinois. Many friends came in the afternoon to wish us well. The line went until six that evening. At about five, our Delavan friends Judge and Beverly Groenewald came to wish us well and Jerry and Callie Hauptli arrived from Phoenix, Arizona. What a surprise moment!

Paula, Scott, Charla, and Thora prepared a skit on our life. It was very funny but well done. Charla was a carpenter with Ray's gear on. Our wonderful friend, Roxanne Michael, took a video of the whole day. She worked very hard, but what a memory it was. Several movies of our days in Papua New Guinea and our wedding day were being shown all day. It was a glorious day! Our hearts were filled with thankfulness and praise to God. He has blessed us so richly, and we are just sinful people, but He choose us to work for Him.

CHAPTER 38

Paula Marries

In 1992, December 12th, our daughter Paula was planning to marry Scott Price, so planning a wedding in the middle of the school year was challenging. She had a beautiful Christmas wedding at St. John's Lutheran Church in New Minden. Ray's sister, Thora (Paula's baptismal sponsor) came for the wedding. Around two hundred guests came and a reception was held in Hoyleton Community Center.

CHAPTER 39

Trinity-Hoffman Continued

I continued teaching at Trinity Hoffman, grades one and two, until 1993 when Ray Richert, our principal, retired. The board of education knew I had been principal before, so they asked if I would be principal. Since Paula and Charla had graduated from Nashville High School, Paula in 1986, and Charla in 1987, and they were now in college at the University of Illinois, Champaign, I decided I could handle being principal. So, then I was principal and teaching half days in grades one and two. Judy Kasten and Joy Michael split the day with me by picking up the afternoon with the children. Again, this was all possible since I had a wonderful God leading me and an excellent secretary, Rita Tyberendt.

I enjoyed my years at Trinity-Hoffman. I had terrific supportive pastors, teachers, and parents to work with. Our students did very well while with us and were doing academically very well at Carlyle High School. We had state inspections every four years, and those always went very well. We had wonderful people in the congregation who helped get the building in top-notch shape; one who was very helpful was a high school friend of mine, Leroy Fruend. Our school was growing, and we were thinking of expanding, but in 1997, I decided to retire.

The congregation gave me a wonderful retirement send-off. There was a church service followed by a dinner at the school. It was another praise God event! We had Rev. Jim Herzog, my mentor from PNG, there to do part of the service. The parents gave me a big basket of flowers and other decorations were all around. My congregations from Levittown and Lincoln also sent flowers, and some of them came for the service. What a glorious day!

CHAPTER 40

Teaching in China

I was planning to go to China that summer in 1997, to teach English as a foreign language. The congregation gave me the money as a farewell gift to pay for my trip, which was such a blessing. I finished the school year at Hoffman. It took a lot of emotional energy to clean out the classroom and office. It was hard to leave teaching as I loved my years in the classroom. I could not thank my God sufficiently for all His blessings.

I prepared to go to China: I had a passport, but needed a visa. I was going with a "Teaching English as a Foreign Language" group from California. I flew to Torrance, California, on June 22nd, and a wonderful group met me. We worshipped at a wonderful church, and they gave us a royal send-off. A lot of prayers were said for us in the service.

This was different again, getting on a flight to China, a Communist country. We landed in Beijing and were set up in a hotel, not like the U.S., but comfortable. I had two roommates. We were scheduled for a week of very helpful orientation. One of the phrases we learned was, "Where they lead you, you will follow. What they feed you, you will swallow." It was good advice as we were watched at all times by the Chinese authorities and were not to talk politics or Christianity. We were divided into teams of 4 or 5 and sent out to different places in China.

At the end of the week, we were assigned our place of work. I was to go to Fuzhou in the southeastern part of China. From Fuzhou, we drove up into the mountains on a terrible road of bumpy and broken concrete. At noon we stopped at a restaurant and were ushered into our own room. We had frog soup, rice, and spicy dishes, and watermelon. Pastor Clarence Budke, who had been in New Guinea with us, was on my team along with Rev. Gerald Lange and Ann Hendrick. Rev. Budke knew how to handle the soup, so he dug out meat for us from the frogs and broth. It was an experience! Rev. Budke had done summer tutoring in China earlier, so he helped us a lot. We got to Yongan at about 6 PM. We went to our hotel and ate supper at the hotel. Always rice with side dishes, very tasty. The first day was orientation, and in the evening, the board of education gave us a seventeen-course dinner and a lot of speeches. We were made to feel very welcome.

The next morning a van picked us up and took us to the school. We had gotten materials at our orientation. Our students were teachers who wanted to learn English to teach their students. Their students could not get into college unless they knew English. Being a first and second-grade teacher, I had them start on learning the alphabet, sounding the vowels and then the consonants, and then putting them together for words. Then it was teaching vocabulary and making sentences. We also did easy poems like "Roses are Red," "Peter Piper Picked a Peck of Pickled Peppers," etc. We had a lot of fun.

We had five weeks with our students, and they got to be like family. They were so kind and eager to learn. They took us to their homes; some had dirt floors, some lived in high-rise apartments: no elevators, so we got our exercise. They took us to the market, and that was exciting and a learning experience. The market had about anything you could think of. There was food, clothing, dishes, pots and pans, jewelry, baby chicks, ducks, and other animals. It was all very inexpensive, although sometimes the merchants would raise the prices for U.S. tourists.

In our Social Studies class, we taught about holidays: Christmas, Easter, etc. and so we could tell them about Jesus. Bibles were not allowed unless they were made by the Amity company and were Chinese stamped. We could not give any to the students.

There was a church a few blocks away, and we went every Sunday. It was an excellent way to witness, but we were not allowed to do any proselytizing. The people at the church made us sit in the front row and brought us tea. The sermons were Christ-centered, and the choir sang Christian hymns. One was "Holy, Holy, Holy, Lord God Almighty." "Kena, Kena, Kena" – I will never forget it – it touched my soul. After each service, we got many hugs; we felt a real bond with them in Jesus, our Savior. To this day, my prayers are for those Christians. Even though they have a hard life and are not accepted in the day-to-day world because of their faith, God is doing great work there, and one day in heaven, we will see them again, praising Jesus together in God's marvelous kingdom.

Before we left, the students had several parties for us. The rooms were always beautifully decorated; they have beautiful colorful paper cuts, hanging ornaments, etc., which made it special. The Board of Education again gave us a seventeen-course farewell dinner. It was royal! We had Peking duck, eel (the whole fish beautifully displayed on a platter), soup, rice, some vegetable dishes, and the last dish was watermelon. Each course was served separately, so it took two to three hours for the meal. Afterward, there were a lot of speeches – they made us feel special. We felt like we only tried to help them and hoped we did.

Then it was time to leave. It was hard. There was a lot of hugging, crying and they gave us gifts like scarves, vases, decorated knives, bookmarks, ornate paper cuts, and more.

Then the ride down the bumpy road to Fuzhou and our flight to Beijing. In Beijing, we had a few days to enjoy sightseeing. We were blessed that a student, Eric Wood (now a Pastor at Immanuel Lutheran, Okawville, IL) who had taught in China three years, was with the group who had completed their teaching. He took us to an acrobat show and a theater presentation performed with precision. We also went to The Great Wall, climbed to the top and what a beautiful view! All along the bottom were many shops for tourists.

Then the long flight to Los Angeles and on to St. Louis. Ray, the Wayne Maschhoff's, and Robert Poirot's were there to meet me. It was a great reunion, and I had so much to tell them.

It was now August, and Trinity-St. John's Lutheran School, Nashville, needed a teacher to teach grades one and two. I was missing teaching, so I accepted and taught there for the 1997 – 1998 school year. I enjoyed the year and had a great principal and staff to work with. My classroom always had live animals so I got a hamster. The children loved him. Sometimes he got out of his cage at night, and we had fun finding him. One day, a student who had a hamster wanted to bring it, so I thought, "Okay, we can handle two cages." However, one Sunday morning, during Sunday School, they decided to put the hamsters together in the same cage. Mind you, a couple of months later, when I came in, we had four babies in one cage! The children loved it, and it gave them excitement for the rest of the year.

We did a lot of singing in the classroom, and could join the school choir under the music teachers Janice Lange and Diane Backs. We sang some Sundays and at our Christmas program. It was a great year, but I really wanted to retire, so I declined to teach another year.

CHAPTER 41

Charla Marries

In 1997, our daughter, Charla, was engaged to Russell Eng-lebretsen, and they were going to be married on June 27th. They were both U of I students, so May and June were filled with wedding preparations. They decided to be married in the pasture behind St. John's-New Minden church. It kept Ray busy cutting grass and getting the grounds ready. He built an altar with a cross on it. Ray's two sisters, Thora Hausler and Joyce Deuble, came out from Australia for the wedding, which added to the excitement.

The wedding day was beautiful. The Maschhoff's, always helping, brought their old truck, beautifully restored, and drove the bride and wedding party to the pasture. It was a beautiful service with Rev. Tim Mueller and Rev. Jim Herzog performing the ceremony. Being out in God's creation made it special. Then we had a reception at Hoyleton Community Center. The cooks, Gerry Schnitker in charge, prepared a wonderful turkey dinner.

After the wedding, Ray and I took his sisters on a trip. We went up to Racine, Wisconsin, for a fellow missionary's daughter's wedding. Then we drove across Wisconsin, Minnesota, the Dakota's, down to Denver, and up the mountain to Westcliffe where I had taught. Texas Creek, where I had, for an hour, sat and waited for the mail wagon, was now a small town! Westcliffe was very much the same, but Silvercliffe was now a booming city because many people were moving out of Denver and Colorado Springs to a quieter area. Then it was down to Mesa Verde and on to Death Valley in Arizona and back across New Mexico, the Texas panhandle, Arkansas, Missouri, and Illinois.

It was a beautiful trip, and they were so happy to see this part of America. The Mesa Verde villages in the mountain cliffs were a good educational preserve of the ancestral Pueblo people, and we learned a lot about how hard life was in early America. Ray's sisters were awed by the Rocky Mountains. The mountains in Australia are not as high as in the U.S. After we got back, it was time to say goodbye to Thora and Joyce, always a teary time.

Chapter 42

Immanuel-Okawville

Then it was back to work, Ray at the prison, and I had been asked to teach at Immanuel Lutheran School, Okawville, Illinois – fifth and sixth grade. Well, I was still missing teaching, so I did it for a year. Again, it was a very pleasant year. Fifth and sixth grade was a little more challenging, but a beautiful group of Christian boys and girls and a wonderful principal, Cora Schmidt.

CHAPTER 43

Passing and a New Role

In October of 1998, my sister Erna passed away from cancer. She had a handicapped daughter, Marcella. Marcella was living at the children's home, Diamond View, in Centralia. My sister, Wilma, and I decided we would take her out once a week for a McDonald's treat, a Pepsi, comics, and a small car as a gift. Wilma passed away in 2013, so I was left with carrying out our commitment. By this time, Ray had retired, and he was taking Wilma's place. The joy it brings Marcella is worth every effort.

CHAPTER 44

Trinity-Hoffman Again

In 2000, Trinity-Hoffman needed a principal after two months of school, so I said I would take over for the year. It was also a year when the state would visit in January. Well, Ray and I had planned to visit his family in Australia for Christmas, so we asked the state to postpone their visit to May, which they did. Once again, I had an excellent staff to work with.

Our trip to Australia was beautiful as it was summer, and they have beautiful flowers, vegetation, and Ray's home near the beach was in a beautiful location. Seeing his family was always special.

When we returned to Hoffman, we continued to get everything at school in order for the state visit. There were some construction issues in the stage area that needed repair. Other things needed updating and touching up. Men of the congregation completed the needed repairs and updates.

We had four men from the state inspect our school in May. Dan Roth, education executive from our Southern Illinois District office, and Rev. Keith Wachter, our pastor, were there with them. Rita Tyberendt, our school secretary was a great help. Thanks to all these efforts, we came through with flying colors.

I enjoyed my years of teaching so much, but now after forty-seven years, I gave it up as our daughter, Charla, and husband Russell were expecting a child, so I wanted to be able to help take care of him.

CHAPTER 45

Visit to Australia

In 2003, we took another trip to Australia. We had wonderful visits with family, many fish and chips (like French fries) dinners, and visits to the beaches. Paula and Scott; Russell and Charla also came. We had such fun doing the Aussie things. Paula and Charla even picked up the Australian accent pretty well. We spent four days at Binnaberra, with Jeff and Helen Ost. It's a resort on the hills south of Brisbane. We lived in cabins and ventured through the forest. We wore hats with tassels with cloth balls all around to keep the mosquitos from eating us too severely. We then decided to take a trip back to Papua New Guinea.

We took the trip to Papua New Guinea with Paula and Scott, and it was emotional for Ray and me; we had so many memories there. We stayed in Lae with one of our students Dian Roo. He took us to see the Martin Luther Seminary and Balob Teachers College we had established there. We were happy to see they still had large numbers of students at each school. Dian also took us to a crocodile slaughterhouse where many crocodiles were kept in ponds to be killed for meat and leather. There is a big market in Japan for them. We saw some beautiful articles made of skins: purses, shoes, bags, etc. It was fascinating, and we ended it with a crocodile dinner, very tasty!

We flew on to Madang, where our mission vacation house is located. As usual, it was a beautiful place. Paula and Scott got to scuba dive and revealed to us how beautiful the sights are under the water. They said it was excellent for diving. We ate at the hotel, which was there when we went there on vacations from Papua New Guinea during our mission work. It was known for good food, atmosphere, and entertainment. A New Guinea band played; some of their instruments were bamboo.

We saw oodles of flying foxes (bats) hanging from trees, which Ray and I didn't remember being there before. The market and vendors were fun for us all, and we bought more locally made items. Their carvings were excellent and beautiful. Then we flew up to Mt. Hagen. Everything looked different and more developed. One of our students, Rasaka, met us with a jeep in Mt. Hagen and drove us to the Western highlands where we had worked. On the way, we slept at a lodge that Dian Roo owned. Pausa looked very different, the buildings needed paint jobs and repair, but the work was going on. It had become a boarding school of one thousand students. The chapel was still there, and the original classrooms, with more classrooms added.

We went on to the hospital run by New Guineans who had been trained by our doctors and nurses. Paula and Charla were born there. Dr. Lutz and his family were there carrying on the work. Dr. Lutz passed away several years later, but his wife and son are still there doing long hours and good work. We only have a small mission staff left there. The head nurse was one of my first students, Kegeme from Raiakama. What joy it was to see her. She gave me a beautiful billum made of wool.

We went on to Kumbasakum, where the business center continues to be run by New Guineans. Then we drove up to Yaibos, where I had stayed my first six months in Papua New Guinea. It is still a mission station. Then we traveled to Amapyoka, our missionary children's school, now a New Guinea school. This is the school where Ray and I were married. We have an excellent Christian New Guinea lady, Pam Lui, who does a wonderful job keeping the school going. She is an excellent teacher. Paula and Scott were all eyes and ears. Such a great experience for them. Paula was four, and Charla was three when we left there, so Paula still had some memory of the area.

We went up to Irelya, still a strong mission station, and across the road is Wabag, which now has a hospital and some businesses, and it is the Highland's government center. It also has an airstrip.

Then we drove back to Mt. Hagen and got a flight to Port Moresby, where we stayed at a hotel. It is the capital of Papua New Guinea, so a lot of people live there. It has shopping areas, churches, adventures on local trips, etc. Several of our students were there, and we had great visits. Then the flight back to Brisbane.

Russell and Charla were there to meet us. They didn't get to go to PNG because Charla was pregnant. They had flown to Ayres Rock and done some sightseeing. The next day we all flew back to the U.S., tired and worn out but so thankful God kept us all safe, and we could make this trip together. We witnessed a lot about our wonderful God, who has blessed us with so much even though we are undeserving sinners.

Ray's siblings: Ray, Thora, Selma, Alva, Joyce sitting

CHAPTER 46

China Again

Ray and I made two trips to China during the summer of 2000 and 2004, teaching English as a foreign language. Our first trip was to Lanzhou in North Central China. I taught teachers, and Ray taught doctors and nurses. We enjoyed our students so much in five weeks; they were like family. We again had Pastor Budke as our leader. We had two other lady teachers and one man.

One of our lady teachers had an appendicitis attack in the middle of the five weeks. Pastor Budke contacted our doctor students in the middle of the night, and they took her to the hospital. It was an "experience" as sanitary conditions were not like in America, but she made it okay. The next morning, we heard about it and had a prayer session, then went to see her on our way to class. Ray and I immediately realized, as in New Guinea, the family takes care of the patient, as she was still in her bloody clothes. Her bandages on her incision looked okay. Later, after class, I had brought along some Clorox from home, and another teacher and I changed her clothes, got clean linens, and scrubbed her bathroom. We cleaned her each of the 5 days she was in the hospital. Then arrangements were made for her to fly home. She made it okay as a medically handicapped patient. She said she had excellent treatment all the way home.

Lanzhou was different from Yongan. Noodles instead of rice is the staple. This is a wheat-growing area. We saw many noodles being made and ate a lot of noodle dishes – especially soup. They served us good meals at the hotel, sometimes things we didn't recognize. On one occasion, Ray asked, "What is this?" and the lady next to him said, "Cat." Sorry, but Ray had to eat it! Anyway, remember: "What they feed me; I will swallow!" Ray and I stayed healthy the entire time we were there.

Lanzhou is on the silk route, a famous trade route from Europe to China. Lanzhou was a significant water source on the Yellow River; it looked very yellow from sand and yellow dirt. When we left, the students again gave us a seventeen-course dinner, and the Board of Education did the same – delicious food served one course at a time. Each dish was beautiful and served elegantly. Peking duck was always one of the courses and eel with the eel cooked in its skin, beautifully displayed with greens, flowers, and cherries around it. We were always glad when the watermelon came as we knew it was the last course, and we were stuffed!

As in Yongan, we went to church every Sunday; they had a beautiful large brick church. We also had devotions every morning at breakfast and prayers in the evening. As we left, we were laden with gifts and a lot of hugs and tears.

We flew Chinese Airlines in China, and they were uncomfortable for Ray as the seats are made for smaller people, and Ray is tall. We flew back to Beijing and did some sightseeing at Tiananmen Square, the Summer Palace, and we went to the Great Wall again and climbed up to the road and walked down it a little way. And again, we saw a lot of shops, souvenirs, clothes, etc. Then we had the long plane ride back to Chicago and a happy reunion with Paula, Charla, and their families.

Our final trip to China was in 2004. We flew from Los Angeles to Guangzhou. Then we flew on to Kunming in southwest China. We were met by a missionary family working there. We stayed three days for orientation. We learned about their missionary work and attended church; it was so full we had to sit on steps going up to the balcony. They gave us newspaper to put under us to protect our clothes as we sat on the steps. One gentleman gave me a seat on a bench. I was sitting next to an elderly lady, and I crossed my legs. She quickly took my leg and put it back as they don't think you should cross your legs; it cripples you. It was interesting to see under what great surveillance our missionaries had to live to work there; even inside their home was a camera.

Then we took a bus on up to Shanyi, the city where we would work. We were a team of five: Alex Opper, Lori Foster, Ann Dennis, Ray, and me. We stayed in a hotel and had to walk ten blocks to the school where we taught. First, we had a week of orientation. It was quite intensive and informative. We trained teachers and sometimes, in the evenings, high school students. We really enjoyed teaching; they were a lively group with much enthusiasm and willingness to learn. Our classes were in a high school building, and we had many steps to walk up to get to our classroom.

Sometimes in the evening and also one afternoon, when I taught high school students, there were ninety or more in the room. Discipline was no worry; they were very attentive, wanting to grasp every word. Sometimes I would break teaching and sing a song like "You Are My Sunshine" or "Row, Row, Row Your Boat," and they loved it and caught on quickly.

There was only one thing I've always regretted. One day they asked me, "What is the reason for your spirit? You are always happy: your face is smiling." I had a perfect chance to tell them that I have Jesus as my Savior in my heart and because He loved me so much, He came into this world and gave His life for me, I am now free of sin, and Jesus' joy makes me happy. You can talk about Jesus if they ask you, but I blew it. I had a whole room of students, I could have given an excellent witness about Jesus, So I've asked Jesus to forgive and pray that our being there and them seeing us go to church, they would make the connection to Jesus being the source of my joy.

In our Social Studies class, we did a Christmas play and Easter play, and we also had a mock Christian wedding. We found a beautiful long white dress in the shop window and bought it for the "bride," and we found a suit for the boy and a dress for the "bridesmaid" and a shirt, tie and pants for the "groomsman." Mr. Opper was the pastor and did such a good job. Of course, this went over superbly with the students: to see an American wedding. The "bride" thanked us many times for her beautiful dress. The ceremony was Christian and about how to live as a Christian man and wife.

We went to church every Sunday, and it was always packed, but they saved a bench in front for us. The service was about 3 hours long, all in Chinese. Again, they brought us tea. The church was so full that they had chairs outside going down the footpath. We got there at 8:30 AM, sang until 9:30 AM, then the service lasted until noon, and at one o'clock, they had a church meeting. They were so happy to be there; their joy filtered into us. We thought, "If only we could get this kind of enthusiasm in our churches in the U.S." But our being there was a comfort for them. It was a reassurance to them of other Christians in the world caring for them.

On one school day, Mrs. Xhi, superintendent, arranged to take us to the country and look at schools there. It was quite an experience. The school rooms only had benches, nothing on the walls to make them cheerful. We saw math and language books, little else.

The roads in the country were in very poor condition. We learned how poor educational conditions were for students, especially in the country. We all felt like we wanted to go home and gather books for them. All in all, we were so thankful to be there to encourage the teachers, help them and give them enthusiasm.

Our last night was spectacular. The Christians had a dinner for us in an upper room at the top of an apartment building. At the dinner, the pastor secretly shared with us that the government was giving them land to build a new church because of our presence. The church they had was a large old shed that they had fixed up with Jesus pictures all around and an altar of wood boards and a small foldup organ. We truly learned "The church is not a building, it's the people." Anyway, the pastor was so excited, and they were ready to start construction right away. After dinner, we went into a large room and sat on benches all around the room. We sang hymns, said prayers, and a few people made speeches about how happy they were that Jesus had brought us there. We were stunned as Mrs. Xhi, superintendent of schools, and a lady policeman who we found out was the person watching us the whole time we were there, were at the party. She was dressed to a "T" in her black uniform. As we left, the entire group walked us down singing. When we got to the street we sang "Now Thank We All Our God" and "Praise God from Whom All Blessings Flow." It was heavenly, and it was hard to come back to earth. We remarked at the time, how surprised we were that this outpouring of praise to God took place in a public setting.

After this teaching tour was finished, Ray and I spent time seeing Xian, where the "Terracotta Warriors" who had been buried under the ground and have now been dug out, were on display. It's a sight to behold. They had still more to dig out. Then we went to visit Amity where the Bibles are produced. We also spent

time in Shanghai and visited our Lutheran school there, supported by our LCMS. It was beautiful, mostly American teachers,
and well supplied with books, equipment, etc. We had to visit
the market and some shops! It was always an exciting experience!
We saw a rug factory where young girls were putting stitches into
beautiful oriental rugs. We also went to a cloisonné factory and
saw them making beautiful vases, pots, and large pots covered
with the beautiful cloisonné material. Our work in China was a
pleasure and gave us a feeling of thankfulness for the little help
and hope we could leave these people. We left with prayers for all
whom we had met.

*Eunice and Ray's Chinese students; they taught them English as
a foreign language. Summer 2004*

CHAPTER 47

Christ Our Rock Lutheran High School

In early 2000, talk started in our congregation at St. John's Lutheran Church in New Minden, Illinois, that we needed a Christian High School for our children. The initial thoughts came from our member Deanna Holm. Soon a group of us took the idea with serious thought. We said, let's ask all the congregations in the area to join us, and then maybe it would be financially feasible. We started regular meetings with people who were on board with the idea. We soon came up with 15 Biblical Reasons for a Lutheran High School:

1. To assist parents in bringing up their children in the faith.

   "Fathers, do not exasperate your children; instead, bring them up in the training and instruction of the Lord." Ephesians 6:4

2. To more fully carry out Christ's command to His Church to feed His lambs.

   "Feed My Lambs,'…Take care of My sheep." John 21:15-16

3. To Grow in God's Word.

   "Grow in the grace and knowledge of our Lord and Savior

Jesus Christ." 2 Peter 3:18 "'Didn't you know I had to be in My Father's house?' ... And Jesus grew in wisdom and stature, and in favor with God and men." Luke 2:49, 52

4. To be guided by God's Word.

"Your word is a lamp to my feet and a light for my path." Psalm 119:105

5. To Reach Out with the Word.

"Therefore go and make disciples of all nations, baptizing them in the name of the Father and of the Son and of the Holy Spirit, and teaching them to obey everything I have commanded you. And surely, I am with you always, to the very end of the age." Matthew 28:18-20

6. To raise up Christian leaders in the congregation.

"The Twelve gathered all the disciples together and said, 'It would not be right for us to neglect the ministry of the word of God in order to wait on tables. Brothers, choose seven men from among you who are known to be full of the Spirit and wisdom. We will turn this responsibility over to them and will give our attention to prayer and the ministry of the word." Acts 6: 24

7. To Send Young Men and Women into Professional Church Work.

"And the things you have heard me say in the presence of many witnesses entrust to reliable men who will also be qualified to teach others." 2 Timothy 2:2

"'Everyone who calls on the name of the Lord will be saved.' How, then, can they call on the one they have not believed in? And how can they believe in the One of whom they have not heard? And how can they hear without someone preaching to them? And how can they preach unless they

179

are sent? As it is written, 'How beautiful are the feet of those who bring good news!'" Romans 10:13-15

"The word of the Lord came to Jonah son of Amittai: 'Go to the great city of Nineveh and preach against it, because its wickedness has come up before Me.'" Jonah 1:1-2

8. To Learn to Live for Christ in Every Vocation.

"And whatever you do, whether in word or deed, do it all in the name of the Lord Jesus, giving thanks to God the Father through Him." Colossians 3:17

"Therefore, I urge you, brothers, in view of God's mercy, to offer your bodies as living sacrifices, holy and pleasing to God—this is your spiritual act of worship. Do not conform any longer to the pattern of this world, but be transformed by the renewing of your mind." Romans 12:1-2

"Whatever your hand finds to do, do it with all your might." Ecclesiastes 9:10

9. To Increase Positive Peer Relationships.

"He who walks with the wise grows wise, but a companion of fools suffers harm." Proverbs 13:20

"Do not let any unwholesome talk come out of your mouths, but only what is helpful for building others up according to their needs, that it may benefit those who listen. Ephesians 4:29

"[God] comforts us in all our troubles, so that we can comfort those in any trouble." 2 Corinthians 1:4

10. To Develop Christian Character.

"Train a child in the way he should go, and when he is old, he will not turn from it." Proverbs 22:6

"Continue in what you have learned and have become convinced of, because you know those from whom you learned it, and how from infancy you have known the Holy Scriptures, which are able to make you wise for salvation through faith in Christ Jesus. All Scripture is God-breathed and is useful for teaching, rebuking, correcting and training in righteousness, so that the man of God may be thoroughly equipped for every good work." 2 Timothy 3:14-17

"How can a young man keep his way pure? By living according to Your word." Psalm 119:9

11. Provide More Intense Christian Mentoring.

"Therefore I urge you to imitate me. For this reason, I am sending to you Timothy, my son whom I love, who is faithful in the Lord. He will remind you of my way of life in Christ Jesus, which agrees with what I teach everywhere in every church." 1 Corinthians 4:16-17

"Remember your leaders, who spoke the word of God to you. Consider the outcome of their way of life and imitate their faith." Hebrews 13:7

12. To Increase Fellowship Among Congregations.

"And now, brothers, we want you to know about the grace that God has given the Macedonian churches. Out of the most severe trial, their overflowing joy and their extreme poverty welled up in rich generosity. For I testify that they gave as much as they were able, and even beyond their ability. Entirely on their own, they urgently pleaded with us for the privilege of sharing in this service to the saints. And gave themselves first to the Lord and then to us in

keeping with God's will." 2 Corinthians 8:1-5

13. To Watch God Effectively Fulfill His Promises for the Next Generation.

"Therefore, my dear brothers, stand firm. Let nothing move you. Always give yourselves fully to the work of the Lord, because you know that your labor in the Lord is not in vain." 1 Corinthians 15:58

"So is My word that goes out from My mouth: It will not return to Me empty, but will accomplish what I desire and achieve the purpose for which I sent it." Isaiah 55:10-11

14. To pursue excellence.

"As iron sharpens iron, so one man sharpens another." Proverbs 27:17

15. To better use the treasures God has entrusted to the Lutheran Church-Missouri Synod.

"The man who had received the five talents brought the other five. 'Master,' he said, 'you entrusted me with five talents. See, I have gained five more." Matthew 25:20

(Bible references from the New International Version.)

Our meetings grew more and more intense. We were initially called the "Upper Kaskaskia Lutheran High School Educational Committee," which later became the "Upper Kaskaskia Lutheran High School Foundation." Eventually, we changed it to Christ Our Rock Lutheran High School. We were struggling at our meetings as this was an enormous undertaking. In one session, the attendees were all very discouraged, and since I had been through starting a school three times – my experience came through, and I told them, "When you are doing something for the Lord, you don't quit. We have an Almighty God who will never let us down if we are sincere in prayer and trust Him and never quit." I talked for about fifteen minutes, and the atmosphere in the room completely changed. A very positive attitude came forth, and plans, vision statements, mission statements, etc., started to flow. This was a "Praise God Night." Only He can inspire and put fire into hearts.

Soon things really started to take shape. Jerry Rakers, a member of Trinity Lutheran Church Hoffman, Illinois, gave us forty-five acres of land next door to Kaskaskia College near Centralia, Illinois. What a blessing!! We could go forth with funding, which was a significant undertaking, and we soon had enough money to start a school. Having no building at present, we rented the First Baptist Church's extra space in Centralia, Illinois. We had called a principal, Mr. Curtis Wudtke, and he accepted the call. He was installed on July 20th, 2003. We had formed committees for many purposes. One was the "Prayer Committee." I volunteered for this and asked if I could get people to commit to pray. Forty-seven people committed to praying for the high school. Every two weeks, I sent out a prayer letter; many people were praying, and things were miraculously happening. That's how God works! I continued my duties until November 17th, 2013, when a tornado took our house, and I had many other priorities to attend to.

Our group of students attending at the Baptist Church were growing, and we knew we needed to start building, which was happening. Funds were coming in! One of the significant contributors was Maschhoff Pork Farms. We started construction and dedicated our "Christ Our Rock Lutheran High School" on April 22nd, 2007. What a beautiful God-filled service it was!

By 2009, we had seventy-two students. The school had seventeen graduates that year. It was a joy to work on our Lord Jesus Christ's special mission with these many dedicated people. Now our prayer is that God will continue to bless Christ Our Rock Lutheran High School. As long as people pray and trust the Lord, all will be well, and our children will grow in knowledge, wisdom, and strong faith in Jesus Christ, our Savior.

CHAPTER 48

South Africa

In 2009, I was serving on the board for South Africa of the Southern Illinois District of the LCMS. I had served on that board for many years, mostly helping the Seminary in Pretoria, but also the Lutheran Church of South Africa. It was brought to our attention that there were two empty school buildings in Soweto, where a Bishop of the church was pastor. Children were being bussed out of the district to another district and getting on the bus at five A.M. for the one-way trip. I thought that if there were two school buildings not being used in Soweto, we should start Christian schools. So, I did a lot of work laying ground work to get these schools into operation. Rev. Timothy Schaar, Southern Illinois District President, was making a trip there for the church's conference. So, we decided I could accompany him and see the area where the schools were located and converse with the Bishop.

I had already gotten to know Rev. Schaar previously so that was helpful. We landed in Johannesburg and Pastor Weber, who was president of the Seminary, was at the airport to meet us and drive us to Pretoria. We stayed with Pastor Weber and saw the area and worshipped at the Seminary. Amazing how I immediately fell into missionary mindset. Besides our focus on starting schools, Reverend and Mrs. Weber took us to a diamond mine. Very interesting: I had never seen so many beautiful diamonds before. We were able to go through the mine and see the whole operation - all was under high security.

From Pretoria we went to Durban where the church was having their conference. It was a seven-hour trip, beautiful scenery all the way. The road was an Interstate and very good. In Durban I stayed with a South African family, Bernie and Ivan Ortman and their son and daughter. We became good friends. We still write to each other. The conference was much like our church conferences in the U.S. I got to know people, especially some women teachers and deaconesses. After the four-day conference we had a church service at the Lutheran Church in Durban, a beautiful large brick church, surrounded by their cemetery and beautiful flowers, like a garden. At the service seven young men from the seminary were ordained as pastors for churches. I guess it was unusual for South Africans to be in the church as it had been a European people's church until Apartheid came in.

After the service I rode with the Bishop and two other men back up to Johannesburg and onto Soweto. I had good learning conversations with the men. Our stop in Johannesburg was interesting as the Bishop took me downtown to see some of the poor areas of the city. Then we drove on to Soweto and I stayed in the home of a lady lawyer, her mother and daughter. It was a beautiful brick home. The mother could tell me stories about how poorly she grew up and how Apartheid was making life better for them.

The next morning the Bishop picked me up and we rode in to the city. He had a church about the size of our early churches in Southern Illinois (early 1900's church structures). I told him he could start a kindergarten class immediately by moving chairs in the back of the church. I had brought a blueprint for starting a school and lots of materials and lesson plans with me. Then we looked at one of the schools. It was a nice brick eight room school and I was awed. I said "Oh this is wonderful, let's get it into operation quickly. I'll be willing to come and help you." I prayed with the Bishop about this wonderful opportunity. I told him to get carpenters, cleaners, and set up a schoolboard and we could get a good start. He sounded excited but he never contacted me when I got back to the U.S. I sent several emails and letters but they were not answered. So, I was disappointed about this venture.

The next morning, I went to worship at his church. The church was packed, chairs were set out the back door onto the lawn. Twelve young people were being confirmed - they were dressed very stylish in black. They answered the catechism questions very well. Everyone wore black, I didn't know this was the custom so I had a red dress on and felt very out of place. They had me talk about the school and my visit there. I got A-1 attention as they were intensely listening to me. A few questions were asked and I led them in singing "Praise God from Whom All Blessings Flow." Then I was ushered to my seat but had to walk up again to put the offering in the plate at the front of the church. I was very self-conscious! The Bishop gave a wonderful Bible based sermon; he was a very forceful speaker. After the service they had a potluck dinner - food was brought by everyone and I tasted some different dishes, all very tasty. Then at two P.M. the Bishop drove me back to the airport. We had a friendly visit and farewell.

I still pray for the church there. They were very good to me and they loved the Lord!

CHAPTER 49

Grandchildren

We settled back into life in the U.S. We stayed active in our church. Our first grandson, Aaron Englebretsen, was born on June 27th, 2004. Aaron kept me busy going up to Chicago on the Illinois Central Railroad from Centralia to Union Station in Chicago, then catching the metro to Westmont where Charla and Russell lived. I continued this for a couple of years. Aaron was a smart bubbly boy who was into Thomas trains. Ray built him a table to put his track on, and he knew every train and everything about Sodor Island. He learned Christian songs quickly, and we had so much joy singing them with gusto. They were close to a park, and we played on swings and slides. We also took walks to see the trains, but he was not so fond of real trains!

The next year, grandson number two, Evan Price, came along. I spent time in St. Charles, where the Prices lived. About this time, Russell stopped working his professional job to become a full-time stay-at-home father, so they did not need me as much at their home. I often drove to St. Charles as it was harder to get to the metro, Oglesby Station from Union Station, going out to St. Charles.

Those years of babysitting our grandsons were very happy. I could teach them, love them, and just enjoy them. Best of all,

I could read them Bible stories and tell them about Jesus, how much He loved them and died for them, so the way to heaven is open for them if they believe in Jesus.

When Evan was two years old, Anna Price was born, so wonderful to have a granddaughter! She fit right in and was an energetic bubble. Ray started going up with me. He made a red wagon for them to ride in. We would pull them down to the Fox River, and they enjoyed throwing little rocks in the river, and black walnuts in fall. They had several black walnut trees in their backyard, so we always had an adequate supply. We'd go to the park next to their yard and play on the swings, slide, etc.

Then Russell and Charla had a son, Nathan. Again, we enjoyed him. He loved their cat, named Turtle, and would hover over him. He was the only one with black hair; the rest were blondes. Two years later, Russell and Charla had a little girl named Carlee. She was special also and was entertained a lot by the other grandchildren. Since Russell was always home, I didn't get to spend as much time with her, but she is an extraordinary smart girl.

All five grandchildren have been a very special part of our life. Ray would make and decorate a cake for each of their birthdays, and we celebrated together. They would each request something special for Ray to make. We had an Elmo, Cardinal, Greased Lightning, Turtle the Cat, and Flower cakes. Always blowing out the candles, eating cake and ice cream, and opening presents was such a joy and would leave us with many happy memories.

One August we were celebrating Paula and Charla's birthdays and the grandchildren found out I also had a birthday and they had no present for me. So, they decided to go to a garage sale down the street and find something. The only one who had money was Evan. He had $20. So, they found a wall hanging which says: "A house is Made of Walls and Beams, A Home is built of Love and Dreams." They paid $5 so each one had to come up with a $1 (to pay Evan back)! They wrapped it beautifully and made Grandma very happy!

Eunice's grandchildren's gift to their grandma for her birthday. They searched the streets in Westmont, Illinois, for a garage sale.

Eunice's grandchildren at St. Louis Science Center getting a "Build a Bear."

Eunice and Ray's family one Easter Sunday

Eunice with her two daughters: Charla (left), Paula (right)

Ray and Eunice with their two girls and their son-in-law's Russell, Charla,
Eunice, Ray, Paula, and Jerry.

Charla graduated with a law degree. She works for Discover. Paula has a degree in architecture- has her own business Batir Archecture.
Paula Price and Charla Englebresten- Eunice and Ray's daughters-November 26, 2016 Toowoomba, Australia
50th Anniversary celebration (paid for by Paula and Charla)

CHAPTER 50

Mission Home

Ray's sister, Thora, came from Australia often to visit us. What a joy for Ray to have her in the U.S. As mentioned earlier, sister Joyce came with her for Russell and Charla's wedding, and we did the tour of the western states together. Since Ray and I always felt our house was a mission house, it is always open to visitors. As Rev. Herzog had made our wedding sermon on this theme, it turned out to be a mission home as he said it should be.

We had many Australian visitors over the years. Ray's friend, Roy Weier, and wife, Shirley, came for a week. His friend, Arthur Schloss, and wife Wilma came, John Kessler and wife Val were here. His brother Alva and wife Noela came also. Their son Greg and wife Elenore came. Our mission friends from Papua New Guinea, Don Jeffers and wife Joy, Clem Janetzki and wife Esmay, Janice Haby, Althea Weier Milbroth, Rev Harry Fruend, and wife Dora came. Many of our friends from Papua New Guinea days, Dian Roo and wife Lean, Jacob Luke and son Israel, Pam Lui, Pastor Patric, and we saw many of our students when they came to the U.S. every other year for our Papua New Guinea Reunion. About fifteen to twenty usually came to thank us for bringing them the Gospel. They gave a tremendous witness to Jesus and brought their guitars to sing Christian songs. This was such a reward and joy for us as missionaries.

Ray and Eunice with the President and Secretary of Gutnius Lutheran Church, Western Highlands, Papua New Guinea when they visited us in 1983.

CHAPTER 51

Australia

In 2009, Ray and I made another trip to Australia, and we had a wonderful visit with family and friends. Russell, Charla, Aaron, Nathan, and Carlee also came. We had many happy occasions. Ray's brother had a home near Coolum Beach. We rented a condo there, and we enjoyed the week so much, except that while Ray was walking on the beach, he stepped on something and had a very infected foot. We couldn't get medical help immediately, so he suffered a lot and has had a bad foot and leg ever since. We did visit friends in Melbourne and Adelaide, but it was hard for him. When we got back to the US, he was in the hospital in Springfield, Illinois, for a week, but with no helpful results.

About this time, our daughter, Paula, was going through a divorce. This was an upsetting time, and we helped her as much as possible. We especially did all we could to take care of Evan and Anna. She was divorced for about five years and then met Jerry Meister. Paula is an architect, and he is a builder, so they work very well together. They had met when Jerry went to her for advice on a project he was building. They were married on the beach of Sanibel Island on July 17th, 2017. It was a beautiful occasion.

A fun dinner party with Ray's family in Australia.

CHAPTER 52

Trials

In May of 2013, my dear sister, Wilma Maschhoff, passed away. She had been a source of strength and encouragement all of my life. Being the oldest girl, she took care of us younger ones in the family a lot. She was always someone I could talk to, and she helped a lot taking care of Paula and Charla when we came back from New Guinea. Together her and I took our niece Marcella out once a week to drive around the country side and have that McDonald's hamburger and ice cream treat!

Then, my brother, Luther, had a heart attack and was in Barnes Hospital, St. Louis, MO for three months. He, Wilma, and I had gotten very close as we were the last ones left of the Richard Redeker family. He died two years later.

Then on November 19th, 2013, we were hit by an EF4 tornado. It completely destroyed our home. It was a shock, but Ray and I had made it to the basement; because he heard the forecast on the television. When we came up, we could see the sky. I looked to the left, and that part of the house was gone. Then I turned to the right, and one wall was standing. On that dining room wall, all pictures were gone except one, a plaque made for me by a 97-year-old gentleman, Adolph Rebstock, which said: "Trust in the Lord." This saying lifted my soul, and I said, "Okay, Lord, I understand, I can take it." So, the Lord strengthened both Ray and me, as we knew the Lord wanted us to witness through this for Him. Well, within an hour, we had so many people around us wanting to help!

Many brought totes and Home Depot sent boxes, brooms, shovels, etc. The media occupied Ray and me while our friends were working. The Wayne Maschhoff family helped so much. They came with trucks and trailers and let us put all the things recovered, in a big shed at their place. Ken, the Maschhoff's son, picked us up about 6 PM and said "I have a house for you." It was right on the corner, a block from our house, furnished, filled with food, so we were well cared for. It was a house they used for their workers but was empty at present. (God providing again)! Wayne and Marlene even lent us their car, a Lincoln Continental. So, we just praised God for all the blessings He was sending our way, even though we weren't comprehending everything, but we were happy inside.

A friend, Wendi Gorney, came with totes and was out picking up some of our possessions strewn around the neighborhood. She found a large plastic girl dressed as a maid, which had been given to Ray by Karen and David Maschhoff when I went to China without him in 1997. She set it up in the ditch and said, "Now you watch over Ray and Eunice." Anyway, the media got a picture of us two, and it hit the news and was all over the US by Monday morning. They featured the "Trust in the Lord" plaque. Wendi's mother was going into heart surgery in Phoenix, Arizona. She saw the paper before she went in to surgery and said, "Well, now I know I'll be okay if they can handle all that!" God is good!

That Sunday evening, the news had spread all over the world. Our students were calling us from Papua New Guinea, as well as friends and family from Australia. What comfort! Many calls came that evening, and the many friends and family who came to visit and help, made us feel very blessed.

Our children arrived from Chicago after their six-hour drive, and they stayed to help for several days. For four days, we had no rain - how good God is! - and people packed up so much that was left. The Orville Heseman children all came to help, and Keith's son Collin, did the final touch of knocking down the few walls still standing. Dennis Knauer took our beat-up china cabinet and later brought it back looking like new. We lost some precious memory things, but it really put our thinking straight – we are only here on earth a short time, heaven is our home.

It took almost four years to get back to normal.

Jack Graham, our insurance agent, and the State Farm Insurance company treated us wonderfully. We built a new house on the same spot. They provided everything we needed, including all the furnishings. Ray and I did a lot of shopping! I did a lot of cleaning insulation out of things that were rescued. We can thank God that we were able to get around good and still work. One day after I had finished cleaning insulation out of a lot of drawers and boxes, we went to the Maschhoff shed, and I looked at the many boxes and things there, and I said, "I just can't clean anymore!" so we asked Mr. Graham if we could get cleaners to help us. He said yes and contacted ServPro for us. They did a fantastic job and returned it to us all sorted and cleaned. All I could do is praise God for all His goodness to us, shown through loving people.

Chapter 53

Fifty Years of Blessings!

In 2016, Ray and I were married 50 years. We weren't sure about celebrating, but our daughters took care of that. Charla paid for our airfare to Australia and back, and Paula paid for a lovely dinner with our family and friends in Toowoomba, Australia. All of Ray's siblings were still alive, and many of our missionary Australian friends came. Ray's special friends, Len Dimmick and Val, and Arthur Schloss and Wilma were there. It was such a happy time. Paula and her family came for the occasion and a visit to Australia. The morning before the event, Charla arrived. She had flown over for the occasion. Our spirits were high, and we had a wonderful celebration day. Our good friend, Jeff Ost, was Master of Ceremonies, and like his father, George, who was one of Ray's best friends but had passed away, he kept the party going with spirited tales, and the whole group had lots of memories to tell. Ray and I had a hard time believing all this was happening to us.

The week after, I went to Melbourne to my special friend's funeral, Reta Wiebe Thiele, who was my travel mate on my world trip. It was sad to let her go as we always called and had so many pleasant conversations. Her children were wonderful to me, and we laid her to rest, knowing we'd see her again in heaven. After I got back, we did some sightseeing with Paula and her family around the Brisbane area. It was a lot of fun at Carubbin Wildlife Sanctuary, where the parrots flew and landed on Evan and Anna's heads. After one landing, Anna put her straw hat on! The staff gave us plates of honey and bread to feed the birds, so sticky feet got on our heads. We also got to see Ray's sister, Joyce, who was in the nursing home. She passed away a short time later.

We attended a church service at St. Andrew's Lutheran church in the middle of Brisbane. It was inspiring that Jeff Ost had a special memorial wall in honor of his parents, Ray's closest friends. It was also an international church with people from many different countries as members.

The next day Helen Ost took us to visit Ray's cousins Ollie and Auburn Mueller, and Glenn and Val Dimmick, Ray's good friend and cousin who had helped Ray in younger days. Our goodbyes were hard as we knew it was our last trip to Australia, and we would not see them again in this world.

After a few days in Toowoomba, saying goodbye to friends and family, Greg and Elenore Hausler, Ray's nephew, came up from Brisbane and then took us to the Brisbane Airport. Our flight home was smooth and uneventful. We both realized the airlines' service was not as exceptional as it had been on our earlier trips, but we were safe and thankful.

Our last six years, since 2014, have been busy at Christ the Vine Lutheran Mission in Aviston, Illinois. We worked closely with visiting Pastors, Gail Klitzing, Pastor and Cathy Scharr, Pastor James and Linda Gullen, Kimberly and Brad Wolter, and Sherry Wessel, who was our organist and like family. We pray that God will continue this mission as we now have added Pastor Rev. Roger Drinnon and his wife Katrina to our group.

Now our life is much slower, and we enjoy our quiet times. We still enjoy visits from family and friends. On our 53rd wedding anniversary, I fell in the kitchen and broke my hip; this was a jolt as I had never had a broken bone. I recovered quickly after a short stay at Carlyle Healthcare Center, where I was treated royally and had lots of visitors and flowers during the Christmas season. My right knee was damaged and I had knee replacement surgery in July. All went well and I am good again!

My prayer is that, as we are in the evening of our life, God will keep us in His loving care and when He is ready for us, He will take us in His arms into our Heavenly Home.

Anna Price with parrots on her head-feeding the parrots honey and bread at Tarango Park near Brisbane, Australia.

Eunice and Ray's 50th Anniversary

Conclusion

I can't thank God enough for choosing me, a poor country girl, and giving me the privilege of serving Him all my life. In each and every step of my life, God was always there, giving me the faith, help, encouragement, and strength that I needed—always putting Christian people around me to encourage me in my faith.

My prayer is that all the people I have been with in this life, especially our children, will join me in heaven. I especially pray for Ray, Paula and Jerry, Charla and Russell, Aaron, Nathan, Carlee, Evan and Anna to keep reading their Bible so the Holy Spirit will continue to fill them with faith in Jesus and wisdom from God's Word. My prayer is that all children will learn to know Jesus and love Him dearly to serve Him surely. I pray that all of my students will be in heaven with me. After teaching children for forty-seven years, I realize how important it is for every child to have a Christian education. After seeing how Jesus loves little children, we must do all we can to lead our children to Him.

Mark 9:36-37 NIV "He took a little child and had him stand among them. Taking him in his arms, he said to them, 'Whoever welcomes on of these little children in my name welcomes me; and whoever welcomes me does not welcome me but the one who sent me.'"

Mark 10:15 "I tell you the truth, anyone who will not receive the kingdom of God like a little child will never enter it."

Luke 9:48 "Then he said to them, 'Whoever welcomes this little child in my name welcomes me; and whoever welcomes me welcomes the one who sent me. For he who is least among you all – he is the greatest.'"

The inscription on my college ring is John 8:31-32 *"If you continue in my word, then you are my disciples indeed. You will know the truth, and the truth will make you free."* It has been my life motto.

Along with it my confirmation verse, Psalm 145:18-19, *"The Lord is nigh unto all them that call upon Him, to all that call upon Him in truth. He will fulfill the desire of them that fear Him. He will also hear their cry and save them."*

And from Revelations 22:19, *"and if any man shall take away from the words of the prophecy of this book, God shall take away his part out of the book of life, and out of the holy city, and from the things which are written in this book."*

John closes the last book of the bible with prayer: *"Amen, even so come Lord Jesus."* We sing *"Savior Hasten Thine Appearing,"* but like the apostle Paul, we know there is still work to do. There is no place for idlers in the Lord's vineyard, and so we carry on, sure of His presence with us, rejoicing in the privilege of working for Him until the evening comes and He Himself rings the bell for quitting time and calls us home to eternal rest.